ONLINE BUSINESS FROM HOME WITH AFFILIATE MARKETING:

Step by step Guide to learn all the Secrets about Affiliate Marketing on the Web. Discover one of the best Ways to create your Passive Income

MARK GROWT

Table of Contents

3

Introduction

You cannot fail to be impressed by the thrilling world of affiliate marketing. Affiliate marketing is a field that gives you the option to promote anything without having to actually own it. The choices you have to work with are endless. The networks and companies you can start an affiliate enterprise with are also diverse. However, you should choose carefully which program will be an asset to you.

In this day and age, having a passive income stream is mandatory. With the rising costs of living and the changing face of the majority of working industries right now, having a passive income stream is smart. Previously, passive income was exclusive to those who were wealthy enough to pay the requirements to start up a passive income source. For example, wealthy business owners would purchase a coffee shop and allow it to be completely run by a team of staff, thus leaving the owner with nothing to do except ensure that the bottom line is increasing each year and earning him or her a passive income. Nowadays, anyone can get into earning a passive income. The great aspect of earning a passive income with affiliate marketing is that it costs you very little to actually get started.

Aside from wisely adding a passive income stream to your income source, affiliate marketing also enables you to do many other things. For example, you can build a name and reputation for yourself through growing your presence online that can actually earn you many wonderful opportunities than those who are unknown. Many affiliate marketers have been offered the opportunity to take their own companies to the next level, to work in great positions within those companies, or even to take all-expenses-paid vacations and have all-expenses-paid experiences from their companies.

The number of opportunities you can earn from affiliate marketing in addition to the passive income stream that you are setting up for yourself makes affiliate marketing almost sound too good to be true for many. For that reason, it makes total sense if you are wondering whether you can actually profit from this strategy. The truth is that the answer cannot be guaranteed by anyone else. The only person who can guarantee your profitability is you.

The information provided in this guide will help you understand what is available on the market and how you can benefit from the world of affiliate marketing. Make sure you use the points in this guide to produce a site that reads well and can be found on a search engine. Don't forget to look at how you can promote a site and how you can reach your customers with sensible keywords.

Chapter 1. Zeroing In On Your Niche

Eternally related to differentiating yourself from the competition is segmentation. You cannot completely differentiate your business without first identifying your market segment. In the language of Internet marketing, that translates to finding your specific niche.

Remember that there may be hundreds of products on ClickBank to promote but you must identify a specific niche of products that work together. For instance, you don't want to sell a graphically intense multiplayer online game along with corporate software, all on the same site or page.

Every entrepreneur must know that a well-diversified or differentiated business that serves a very specific segment of the market (i.e. a very specific niche) is more likely to succeed in the long run compared to a business that tries to serve everything to everybody. Identifying your market segment and differentiating your business accordingly gives your business a degree of character, which later on becomes something that your particular business becomes known for.

So, next time you visit the pages of ClickBank, find a set of products that are related that also serve a particular niche. Find keywords that you can use that are related to those products, as well as key search terms that people actually use when they look for similar products that you intend to market.

To Do:

1. Choose A Specific Niche (e.g. Relationships, Health, or Vegetarian Diets) – and choose a niche you like to keep your interest and motivation up. After you've selected a niche, go ahead and select a popular product in your niche.

2. Choose A Product As soon as you create a Clickbank account you can look through Clickbank Marketplace to determine which products fit in your niche. Most of the products are e-books, video, and audio files. The first products listed are the most popular- by default. It will also tell you how much you will make for each sale, and the average rebill total if it's a recurring sale. In addition you can view the gravity, which is very important. The higher the gravity number, the more popular the product – hence, the more sales it's making. A low gravity number means (such as below 5) that the product isn't very popular and people aren't promoting it – this is usually because it's not a good product. Therefore, when choosing a product to sell, you'll want to lean towards products with a higher gravity.

Go ahead and check out a few of the websites listed to see if one of the products catches your eye. Once you've chosen a product, you'll want to check its credibility, reliability, and quality. This is where customer reviews can come in handy. So go ahead and Google search for customer reviews of your product.

Casting Your Line with a Lure

It's commonplace that before you can sell something to people you must first give them something for free. One good strategy that is used by some food stores (or any new business establishments) is that they give away free samples of their products. It actually does two things:

(1) It advertises and spreads word about the new establishment; and

(2) The free gift is a way to lure potential customers into the store.

Translating That Concept in ClickBank Marketing

Now how do you translate that concept in terms of online marketing? Here's how to make money with ClickBank using that very concept. The idea is to give them something that they will perceive as valuable or something that is actually valuable to them. The free gift is declared free, but it actually is traded for something – your prospect's email address. It's actually a fair trade, come to think of it. Both parties get something that is valuable to them.

There was an online marketer who raffled off iPads to prospective customers in exchange for their emails and referrals. He was able to gather thousands of emails in the process. Guess what, other marketers followed suit trying to mimic the strategy and also trying to obtain the same level of success.

You don't really have to spend a lot of money just to give away something for free that can be valuable to your prospective clients. But if you have the funds to give away, then by all means, give away free iPads.

There is another alternative that other marketers use, which is not as expensive. That is by giving away a free eBook. An eBook, a free one at that, is also perceived as equally important or just valuable as any high tech gizmo on the planet. Information is usually a prized possession, especially in the Information Age.

The eBook that you will be giving away for free will be talking about your selected niche. You may include some of the products that you are marketing in the eBook. For instance, if you're selected niche is about MMORPG games and tutorials then you can advertise some games in the book and direct some traffic to your site or directly to a sales page.

Take note that you don't have to write the eBook yourself. You can hire a ghostwriter to write the eBook for you. It will save you the time and effort. Hiring a virtual assistant writer to make you an eBook will allow you to focus your energies on more important matters. The important thing is that you leave precise instructions for your writer to follow. Refer back to and you'll find a ton of websites which you can find writers on.

Note that your free eBook doesn't have to be 100 pages long. It can be as short as 20 pages or as much as 50 to 60 pages long.

Anything longer will be too costly for you or would be just too time consuming. The important thing is that the book should cover exactly the niche of ClickBank products that you intend to market.

Remember that the information in your eBook should be worth the information that your prospects are giving you. They are allowing you to talk to them even further down the line and perhaps convert page visits to actual sales in the near future. If you intend to write the eBook yourself, make sure you cover enough about the niche that it will bring the reader some value.

Creating a Squeeze Page to Build an Email List

You don't have to dedicate an entire website to gather prospective client emails. You can create a one page squeeze page or landing page. The main idea behind a squeeze page is to make your eBook convincing enough so that its visitors will be willing enough to give you their email addresses.

The emails that you gather from the squeeze page will be added to your email list. The conversion rate of these opt in pages will vary greatly. Some of these landing pages convert as few as five percent of its visitors. On the other hand, there are squeeze pages that convert up to 60% of its visitors.

Remember that the goal here is not to sell anything. The goal is to make your page's visitors provide you with the key to reach them in the future. Call it a Trojan horse but hey, you're giving away something that your prospects can actually use. In that regard, this marketing tool is neither deceptive nor abusive in nature since it is mutually beneficial.

Driving the Traffic Home

There are two ways to drive traffic and let people click the affiliate links you posted and eventually earn your commissions. The first way to do it is by getting generic searches from online search engines.

Both methods work. However, many experts and big names in online marketing have said time and again that the money is in the mailing list. Affiliate marketing A-list folks like Shoemoney (he launched what is known in ClickBank as the Shoemoney System), John Reese, John Chow, and also Frank Kern have used and continue to use mailing lists. That is one of their secrets on how to make money with ClickBank.

When you depend on generic searches from search engines you basically create pages and use search engine optimization to your advantage. It's like casting your lines into the water with the bait in it. You end up waiting for the fish to come to you and eventually take a bite. The mailing list approach sort of spins things around because you are the one who comes to the market and tries to lure the fish closer until you eventually catch one.

You can try either one or you can try both. However, experience has shown that the more experienced and successful online marketers definitely build their customer base along with their mailing list. The main advantage of a mailing list is that you already have a captive audience.

One way or another they somehow, to certain degree, know your brand and have trust in your business (even though at times there is just a little amount of trust in there). You have already proven your usefulness, provided that the free eBook you gave was really useful to them. If they like your eBook then they will enjoy the stuff you say in your mails. That will eventually lead to conversions which means you get an eventual sale.

Building Your Mailing List

The fastest way to drive traffic into your squeeze page is nothing more than paid advertising. In the world of Internet marketing, it means that you will pay for pay per click (PPC) and pay per view (PPV) advertising.

There are lots of outfits that offer these services. But finding them is the least of your worries. They are effective, yes, but there is a limit to that. You can see it as a well. One day it will dry up. It will work for a time letting you reel in decent amounts (sometimes really big amounts) of money.

Freebies To Give Away in Exchange for Email Addresses

There are other ways to getting traffic to your site and there are things that you can give away to make people want to trade their email addresses with you. Some experts at certain fields offer free passes to their webinars where they talk about topics that fall within their respective fields of study (aka their niche).

The webinars are free but the attendees are required to sign up for their mailing list. That means they visit the squeeze page or landing page you made and leave their email addresses at the door. Webinars also allow you to interact directly (live!) with your prospective clients. They can immediately tell through this experience if you are really worth their time and money.

Now, you don't have to be the expert that does the talking during these webinars. You can actually hire one for a fee. If it works, that one-time fee you pay the expert to spill the beans in your selected niche will pay off several times in the future since you can use the email addresses that you have gathered in different online marketing campaigns. There is more than one way to milk the cow, metaphorically speaking.

Other than eBooks and webinars, there are other things that you can offer that will be of value to your prospective repeat customers. If your niche is about music then you can give away free music. For instance, if your market segment is about people who are new to guitar playing then you can send short training videos on guitar playing basics.

Within the short training video you can offer even more intense training material that they will have to pay for of course. But the initial training video will be free and all they need to part with in the process is their email addresses. If training videos aren't your thing or you're slightly camera shy then you can just make an audiobook and give it away. If your voice sounds not very appealing then hire someone to read your material and record it.

The important thing is that you are able to think out of the box and give something away that contains material related to your niche.

Build Your Customer Relationship

You can call this the secret ingredient of the secret sauce of every successful person who has learned how to make money with ClickBank or any other online marketing outfit. You see, some people have built lists of up to 40,000 email addresses and still make small profit. There are online marketers who are only able to build shorter email address lists, perhaps just around 10,000 email addresses, and make six figure sales.

The big difference is that the successful ones are those who are able to build their relationship with their customers. This is why it has been stated in the beginning of this book that you should never underestimate the value of a repeat customer.

The first step to do this is to build your relationship with the people who subscribed to you (i.e. the people who traded their email addresses for the eBook or any other freebie that you gave away). You already have their email addresses and it's now time to put that into use.

Using Auto Responders

One of the tools of the trade is using auto responders. These are emails that are sent out at different dates and at different intervals. These auto responders help to build that subtle relationship with your prospective clients. Other than that, they are also promotional materials that remind your customer base about your blog or squeeze page or website.

Other than promoting your particular brand, they are also marketing tools that can be used to market the ClickBank products in your niche that may help cover their needs or solve their problems. I suggest that you send these promotional emails some time later. The first emails should be the ones that build rapport with your customer base.

Remember that customers don't always buy things during their first visit to your squeeze page or even in the first email that you sent them. Continue to give your prospects things that will be valuable to them through your emails. This means that you don't throw in your sales pitch at the start. Do that later when they have learned to trust you and your brand.

Now, crafting these emails is a work of art in itself. They are also one of those tools that have a double edge. It can make or break your customer base. So, I suggest that if you lack the skills to write crafty emails then hire someone to write them for you. It may cost you some money but you will get a lot in return.

One important reminder here is that you should also allow the people in your list to opt out of the program. This means that if they want to get their email address off your list then allow them to do so. This will help you to keep only customers to your target market in your database.

Chapter 2. Building Your Eco-System

In this section, you will learn about the ideal platforms for affiliate marketing, things to keep in mind when you opt for social media marketing, and tips to create lead magnets.

Affiliate Websites

Amazon Associates

Amazon is one of the most popular websites these days. It is an online marketplace that connects buyers and sellers. You can pretty much buy anything under the sun on Amazon. In fact, you can order anything from candy to electronic gadgets. It offers great niche markets and, therefore, it is an ideal space to start an affiliate marketing venture.

Pros:

It offers up to 10% on any product sale that is directed from your link. You can generate affiliate revenue from all the purchases that the referred traffic makes even if it is not directly from the product you are linked to. It is a one-stop shop for a lot of people and offers a massive selection of diverse products.

Cons:

The affiliate cookies generated on Amazon last for only 24-hours. If the referred traffic comes and makes a purchase after 24-hours, you will not earn anything. There are limited options for payout like cheque, bank transfers, or Amazon gift cards.

ShareASale Affiliates

It has been in business for about 17 years and it is certainly updated with all the tech advancements. It is a marketplace for merchants and caters to everything that you can think of. Therefore, there will always be some product or other that you can promote as an affiliate.

Pros:

It offers different payout options like digital payments. There is a wide selection of products available. So, you have the option to pick a profitable product to work with.

Cons:

On the downside, it is not as straightforward as its competitors. It is not a major drawback, but you need a little technical knowledge to work with this platform.

eBay Partners

eBay is a user-based marketplace and you can use it to advertise and sell items on this platform. All that you need to do is find some listings that interest you and then you need to promote them using eBay's Partner Network to get paid for your work.

Pros:

There is no other marketplace on the Internet that offers the diversification that eBay does. You can pretty much sell any legal product that you can think of and no other platform can compete with eBay on the product diversification it offers. There are no technical or complex rules that you need to follow when you use eBay. You need to promote a product, and whenever someone buys using the link you promote, you earn revenue. It also offers a double commission for the first three months you are enlisted with this service.

Cons:

If a specific auction exceeds ten days, then you will not earn anything. There are three parties involved on this platform: you, eBay, and the affiliate. It means that the sales revenue will be split three ways. You will earn a percentage of what eBay will earn from the sale on its site.

Shopify Affiliate Program

One of the leading eCommerce platforms available is Shopify. If you have a niche audience, then this is the perfect platform to cater to their needs.

Pros:

You earn per referral that you make. During the first two months of the referral's subscription fee, you can earn up to 200% of the subscription fee you pay. It is a great platform to earn from referrals. In fact, you will earn per referral.

Cons:

Shopify is an ideal platform only if you are into a niche product. You need a specific audience to cater to and only then it will make sense to use Shopify.

Clickbank

This platform is quite similar to ShareASale. It is a diverse marketplace that is full of merchants from which you can pick something to promote. The merchant you decide to promote will depend on your target audience.

Pros:

It is quite likely that you will find some product or other to promote, given their vast product database.

Cons:

On the downside, they don't have any option for digital modes of payment. The only payment options they offer are cheque, direct deposit, or wire transfers. Regardless of the product you decide to promote, you cannot earn more than $150 per referral sale that is made.

Rakuten Marketing Affiliates

It is an online store that stocks everything from high-priced electronics to pet supplies. If you need something, it is quite likely that you can find it listed on Rakuten. The best part about using this platform is that they will pay you when you help them sell anything on their store.

Pros:

It is one of the most trusted online marketplaces. In fact, it has partnerships with well-established brands like NBA.

Cons:

You will need to individually apply to all the brands that you want to promote. It might take a little extra time, but then again, it does make sense to be prudent about the products you decide to promote. The knowledge base that it offers is difficult to navigate, but they do have a good affiliate support team in place.

Leadpages Partner Program

It is a powerful tool for online marketing. Every individual, regardless of their level of expertise, has the opportunity to create landing pages that help with conversions. The products they offer are unrivaled in their space. If you have a digital audience you want to cater to, then you must consider this platform.

Pros:

If you have the right audience, then it pretty much sells itself. The team at Leadpages does a good job with their products that you merely need to show those with websites that the tools exist to get sales. It is powerful and is certainly worth promoting. Also, they offer a commission of up to 30% on referral sales.

Cons:

On the downside, it might be too niche for a lot of affiliate marketers to work with. It sells well, but it will only sell to an audience who are trying to achieve something from their respective websites.

StudioPress Affiliate Website

It is a niche website, but it is certainly worthwhile if you have a good digital audience presence. This website helps create responsive, adaptable, and customizable WordPress hosting and themes that increase the function as well as accessibility of WordPress.

Pros:

It is another product that tends to sell itself. Most WordPress users need to just take one look at the tools this website offers and all that they can achieve with it. It does make your job significantly easier.

The payouts they offer are quite generous and you can get up to 35% per theme sale and a minimum of $75 per site sale that you make.

Cons:

The only problem with this platform is that it is quite a niche. It will benefit your audience only if they want to establish an online presence for themselves.

CJ Affiliate Publisher's Program

It is a platform that certainly knows what they are all about. They have been in the industry of affiliate marketing for over 19 years now. It will be quite difficult to find any fault with this program, given that they have products in every niche that you can think of.

Pros:

It is one of the largest networks of affiliates and it is difficult to rival them in size. If they have been in business for as long as they have been, then it does make them an expert.

Cons:

The process of application is quite difficult, and it is quite scrutinous.

Picking the Right Affiliate Program

Now that we've gone into the list of reputed affiliate networks it's important to know how to choose an affiliate program that's good for you. All affiliate programs are different and you need to thoroughly inspect each one before you decide to jump into a deal. This section will cover the various things that you need to keep in my mind when finding the program that's the right fit for you.

Terms and Conditions

If you have decided on which company is best for you and your customers, it's time to talk about terms. After all, that's what it's all about. The first thing to ask is how the program works. Are you paid purely for sales, or do you get a commission for leads? It is always better to argue for the latter as you will be tying up with someone who is considering you for your popularity. So, it is a good idea to optimally use this opportunity and argue in your favor. It can make a big difference when it comes down to dollars, both in the amount you can expect to earn, and how long you will have to wait to get paid.

How often do you get paid, and what is the minimum payout level? Many companies pay at the beginning or end of the month, or they may pay out twice a month – usually on the 15th and last day of the month. If you have a certain preference, then you can consider asking them to change the date of payout. Check that the minimum payment threshold is not set too high. Obviously, it's not cost effective to pay out every time somebody clears $10, but if you have to rack up $100 or more before you see the color of your commission, it can be very de-motivating, unless you have a high conversion rate.

Finally, you need to know the rate of commission – both the bottom line and the structure. Some businesses operate a two-tier system, where you get paid for everyone who clicks through to your affiliate, and then receive a further commission if they complete a purchase. Other businesses just pay for one or the other. Commission rates for affiliates vary considerably, from less than one percent for clicks to as much as 75% for some digital download products.

However, it's more realistic to work on a figure between 5% and 20%, and it's worth comparing similar companies to see if their commission rates and terms and conditions are similar.

Remember that money is important, but you will also have to consider several other factors that will help you judge whether the products and services offered comply with your standards. You cannot simply give anybody a nod and must lay down some ground rules for them. This might seem like the wrong thing to do but you need to maintain the standard of your blog and website as well. For this, you can send them a mail, listing the things that you will not be okay with on your blog or site, such as sexually explicit content, weapons, adult products, etc. There are companies who will be looking for people that are interested in letting out some space for such items. So, it is important for you to try to check everything that they send across, just to be cautious.

You must also discuss the rights and obligations and agree upon a termination clause. Remember, if you follow a path that is extremely professional, then it will be easy for you. You cannot take anything too lightly or casually, especially during the initial stages. Make sure you have everything signed and attested just to maintain an official record of your alliance and agreement. Once you are satisfied with everything and have made up your mind to go ahead with the deal then there must be nothing in the way to stop you.

Avoid Paid-for Programs

When you type 'Affiliate Marketing Programs' into Google, you will be inundated with hits. Some of these will be companies who ask you to pay to join their program. They will make use of fancy pamphlets that you can download and mention a well thought out payment plan. What's more, they will probably offer you a huge 'discount' to climb on board. The program's normal sign up cost is $99, but for today only, you will be admitted for the special price of just $20 – it may even be less than that. They will, in fact, make it look extremely attractive by canceling out the $99 with a big red cross and write $20 only next to it. All you have to do now is close the window and move away from such programs.

It goes without saying that there are a million suspicious websites out there, all of whom promise you something but do something else. Now, not saying that these people might cheat you, but even if they are to charge you a high amount of money it will be for their profit and they will not be bothered about you or your website. So don't trust these and only trust your instincts in doing the right thing.

As has already been noted, the affiliate business doesn't pay any commission to you until they make a sale, and remember this is a sale they wouldn't ace without your help. So why would they want you to pay for the privilege of widening their retail reach? That's like saying Microsoft wants to hire you but you need to pay the fees for it.

It can sometimes feel like the right choice to make, especially if the website you visited is promising you many things. I am sure you have also considered it many times just to get started with affiliate marketing at the earliest. You must be more patient when it comes to affiliate marketing, because otherwise, you might end up getting scammed.

But who in their right senses will use their credit card details or check into their online banking account to transfer money to a suspicious source? Not only is it dangerous for your account, but what if you end up the victim of identity theft?

So, as a rule of thumb, don't trust any website on affiliate marketing that promises you good business if you pay them some money first. That is not how it works, and you will have to find a different way in order for you to establish a proper affiliate marketing set up.

Remember, if you stay too long on a website you will be tempted to check it out in detail. Instead, choose to exit as soon as possible and also clear your cookies.

Another thing that happens is that companies charge affiliates to join deals in high-ticket items. You may make a tasty profit from each conversion, but realistically are the people who will be visiting your site going to be interested in high-ticket stuff, even if it is linked to your niche? Even if you can answer 'yes' to that one, you're a beginner in the affiliate marketing game. Isn't it better to make your mistakes for free?

Chapter 3. Finding The Best Affiliate Product Or Service For You

By now, we have read on the things you need to consider when you wish to start affiliate marketing. Now, let us shift focus to the types of affiliate options that are available in the market and the ones that will suit your blog or site the best. Let us look at these in detail.

The best affiliate product or service for you depends on your interests, your niche and your personality. When making your choice, bear in mind that if you have an interest in what you're marketing, you'll enjoy promoting it so much more. It's no good affiliating to a poker website, for example, if you have no interest in gaming, just because the commission is good. When there are problems – and there are bound to be – you'll be more motivated to work through them if you have a genuine interest in the product or service. In that, you can consider promoting two or more products but remember to limit it to not any more than 3 or 4 at a time. Once you identify the best from the lot, you can stick to that one alone and terminate contract with others. These are some of the most popular affiliate programs.

Health and beauty affiliates

Health and beauty is a good niche to affiliate in, because although most of the products are not high ticket, you have the benefit of returning purchasers, so it's possible to build up a decent passive income in this niche.

It is no secret that the beauty industry has seen a considerable boom in the last few years. This is mainly because everybody has become beauty conscious and is constantly trying to improve their looks. It is obvious that they will need cosmetics for their up keep and for this; they will need information on the products.

So, if your blog is about weight loss, healthy eating, fitness or skin care, check out affiliates such as the Market Health Network, which pays a 50% commission on all sales, including recurring sales. Market Health sells natural health and beauty products including skin care products, vitamin supplements, oral hygiene products, and many more, through its various affiliate programs.

This will allow you to write on diverse topics and cut down on the monotony. Imagine what would happen if you have to write on the same topic all the time, it will end you reducing your creativity. But if you spread out your content and write on a diverse range of topics then you will have the chance to showcase your writing talent and impress a large audience. It is also a good idea to check out their products first yourself so that your readers will gain confidence. You can choose a particular product and test it out for your audience. You can click pictures of the product and also the review for it. This will help you connect to your audience better and it will make it easier for you to promote your affiliate links.

Also, Market Health's cookies last for 30 days, so if one of your click-through doesn't complete the purchase but returns to order within 30 days, you'll still snag the commission. Amazon's cookies only last for 24 hours, so you may lose the sale if they don't order right away. Other companies worth investigating are Bath-and-Body.com, which stores cookies for 90 days – one of the longest periods - MedStore online pharmacy and free Weight Loss.com, which offers 50% commission on sales. Remember, if you have heard about the brand then chances are a majority of your readers will also have heard of it. When it comes to beauty products, people generally wish to settle for brands that they have heard about, as it is safer to choose products that they know are reputed. So if you affiliate with some of the best brands then you are in it for the win.

However, if the brand is not really well known but there are a few who vouch for their effectiveness in skin or hair care then you can take the responsibility of making them look good and promote them to your readers. In fact, take it up as a challenge to promote a brand that is not really well known, as it will help you explore your writing and promoting prowess.

You can also have a fashion blog and make it your parallel blog. A lot of the clothing companies and also online clothing stores offer good commission to their affiliates. All you have to do is write on fashion and throw in a couple of pics to help you connect visually. You can promote products of brands that you personally use. As soon as you buy a product, review it and put links. With time, your merchant will be happy with the business that you are creating and might promote you to super affiliate status.

But make sure that the new brand is not your only affiliate as that might retard your growth. Mix it up and have one big brand like The Body Shop and one new company and write about both in the same breath. This will help people relate the two and will consider clicking on the other affiliates ads as well.

Forex (foreign exchange) affiliates

When people think of starting blogs, there are a few standard paths that they take up. One such path is that of writing about travelling and blogging about new destinations to explore. For this, foreign exchange can be a lucrative choice.

Foreign exchange is big business these days. Everybody is now going global and it is possible to reach out to a wide audience by working on this topic. If you run a travel blog, maybe this is the right affiliate partner for you, and the commissions can be very lucrative.

Some forex affiliates trade as a club, and you may have to pay a membership fee, but with commissions ranging from $150 to $600+ per conversion, many people are happy to take that step mainly because of the high rate of returns that it offers. Remember, if there is a guarantee on something then it is worth considering. The only reason that they ask for it is for the upkeep of their club, and so that, you can continue with endorsing them

Forex Club pays a minimum of $200 per conversion and up to $300, and their cookies never expire. Forex Mentor pays 30% commission on every sale and cookies last for 60 days. So it is best to consider this option if you are in it for the long run.

But there is a problem here, many people wonder if they will be able to weave in forex into their travel blogs and wonder if they can promote it effectively. However, there is no need to worry about forex, as you don't have to be a person of finance to understand it. It is easy for you to write about it and all you have to do is sprinkle the links all over your blog.

And if you really happen to be a person of finance then it will prove to be extremely easy for you. There is a chance for you to provide people with information on the basics of foreign exchange and can also be available to solve their problems and answer their queries. Your blog can turn popular in no time, as there is a demand for people who can provide expert views and analysis. Your forex link ups can prosper if you put in the effort to speak about the technicalities of a certain subject and give people a chance to understand the intricacies of the trade.

You can also promote parallel forex trades such as traveler's checks and give an in depth view of what these are. The final goal is to educate the masses on the subject and make sure that they fully understand and click on the ad to derive a purpose out of it.

Food industry affiliates

The food industry is now booming. Right from ready to eat snacks to exotic ingredients, there are a lot of choices in terms affiliate marketing.

People are ready to buy anything that they think will give them a unique culinary experience. Add to it information being provided on what is best to be consumed and how it can be used.

So if you are a food blogger then it is best to tie up with food related companies. There is a wide choice available and you can choose a company that works best with the kind of food that you promote.

Pinch of yum is a good company to consider as they pay 50% commission to their affiliates. It will come as no surprise that the company now thrives thanks to the affiliations that it has with bloggers and website owners.

As long as you have good numbers for your blog, big companies will come rolling in through the door. You can approach big companies such as nestle if you are using a majority of their products in your recipes.

The same extends to Pillsbury, who might affiliate with your blog if it has to do with baking. As long as your affiliates make sense and you do a good job at promoting them on your blog, you are sure to experience elevated sales and inflated commissions.

You need not always blog about recipes alone and can also do restaurant reviews and other such things that are food related. You can also affiliate with restaurant chains that will pay you a commission depending on how many people visit them or order from them.

Online dating affiliates

I'm sure many of you will not consider this and move to the next option. This is mainly because of the stigma associated with promoting a site that caters to dating or making two strangers meet. But hey, everybody needs a partner and if you are helping them in finding theirs then there is nothing wrong with it.

Internet dating is big business, and if you host a relationship or self-help blog, this could be a suitable affiliate partner for you. There is a lot of demand for blogs that give away relationship advice and those that help individuals connect to others in a proper way. It might seem like a rudimentary emotion to fall in love, but some people have a tough time with it. Such people are sure to turn to blogs to seek answers.

If you convince them enough into listening to you and buying products or services that will help them in the process, then you are sure to make your online dating affiliates work in your favor.

E-Harmony is one of the biggest players in the dating game, and it pays up to $188 for every signup. Other dating affiliates to look at are Pull Your Ex Back, which pays up to $128 per conversion, and Kasidie, a swingers affiliate that pays 35% commission for each month your referees remain members. This would be a good fit for an erotic fiction website, or a blog about sexual experiences.

There is no need to worry about your blog being pulled down. As long as you have the permission and advisories in place nobody can touch your blog. So, don't allow any kind of fear to affect you and continue with educating the world. It is possible for you to be as creative as is required and remember, when it comes to fiction, you can go all out and make it as interesting as possible.

You need to, however, know the best places to add in the links, as it will be detrimental to your business. Placing the links at the wrong spots or not making it clear might cost you. So, understand the business first and then weave it into your blog.

Psychic and astrology affiliates

Till now, we looked at things that are quite common and something that most people wish to have but now, we look at something that is slightly off beat.

It is possible for you to have a large base that is only there because you are offering them something unique, which they might not find anywhere else. For this, choosing a topic like astrology can work to your advantage.

You'd be amazed how many people go in for this, so it's a good niche to get into. If you host a New Age or pagan blog, this kind of affiliate would make a good partner, and they pay pretty well too. Psychic Source offers psychic readings and pays a flat commission of $100 per sale. Kasamba is a long established company providing tarot readings, astrological forecasts and psychic readings. They pay up to $150 per referral.

All you have to do is write on the topic in detail in order for people to understand what it is that you are talking about. They should have a good idea about what they are getting themselves into. But just the fact that they have chosen to check your blog out is enough to prove their interest in it. So, try and make the most of it and guide them towards psychic reading.

If you decide to go with this type of affiliate, it's very important to check out the credibility of the individual or company – even more so than normal, due to the nature of the service. Look at online reviews, and if there are a lot of negative ones, try another company.

Online gaming affiliates

Gaming has taken center stage and is something that is enjoyed by one and all. It is always a good idea to consider affiliating with gaming portals as they attract a lot of clicks.

Most online gaming is big business, whether it's poker, casino games or bingo. And the commissions for affiliates are particularly generous. If you host a gaming blog, you may want to link with one of these. Ignite Bingo offers a generous 66% revenue share to affiliates for the first 6 months, then there's a tiered commission system with the best affiliates taking 50%.

Poker Strategy is an online poker school paying up to $500 per referral, with a two-tier commission system. Best Pay Partners is a virtual casino affiliate paying 50% of revenue share, plus 5% for referrals on a two-tier system.

These are just some of the most popular and generous affiliate marketing programs around, but there are many, many more, covering a wide range of specialist niches. Whatever your area of interest, there is sure to be an affiliate marketing network that is a good fit for you, so take some time to do your research and check out all the options available to you.

You can decide to dedicate different blogs to different games. You can concentrate on one genre each and reach out to a bigger audience. As long as you have enough people reading, you will be in a good position to get at least half of them click on the ads. Make sure you make use of simple language so that they understand what you are talking about. But if you are addressing an experienced gaming crowd then make use of gaming terminologies to help them connect with you better.

Chapter 4. Amazon Affiliate Program

On many occasions, people who are new to affiliate marketing are often advised to start with Amazon affiliate marketing for various reasons. With Amazon affiliate marketing, you could easily learn the rope of affiliate marketing and then move on to join the other affiliate networks and grow your tentacles as an internet marketer.

What is Amazon affiliate program?

Just like many other companies, Amazon has since realized that for them to make more money without necessarily increasing their marketing budget; they need to recruit affiliates to do marketing on their behalf.

For companies like Amazon, they know that if an affiliate marketer helps to sell their products, Amazon will earn from the efforts of the affiliate marketer whereas if the company does not give an affiliate marketer an opportunity, the company might earn less. So, Amazon prefers to give affiliate marketers a chance to make money for both themselves and Amazon.

Anyone can join Amazon affiliate program, promote any of the numerous products that are for sale on the Amazon marketplace, and earn a commission. Primarily, Amazon affiliate program was developed by Amazon to allow interested parties to make money from promoting the products on sale on the Amazon marketplace.

Why affiliate marketing beginners should join Amazon affiliate program

There are thousands of affiliate programs out there for an affiliate marketer to join – however, as a new affiliate marketer, you are often advised to start with Amazon affiliate marketing program, and the reasons for that are too numerous to mention – in the following paragraphs, we shall look at some of them.

1. Amazon is a strong brand, and this will rub off on you

Amazon is one of the largest online marketplaces – the internet giant has done a good job of getting their branding right. One problem that most affiliate marketers do face is that they find it hard to convince prospects that the products they are promoting are genuine or original. This is a huge problem because prospects do not want to spend scarce resources on products that will not meet their standards.

To overcome the above problem, affiliate marketers, many times have to spend a lot of time trying to convince their audience or prospective customers that the products the affiliate marketer is pitching are of good quality. Many times, the affiliate marketer has to use various marketing methods like sending emails to convince the prospective client. The affiliate marketer may sometimes have to provide testimonials, social proof, etc.

The affiliate marketer does all of that, especially when they are promoting products that are not well known or when they join affiliate programs of companies that are not well recognized. As an Amazon affiliate marketer, you don't have to face such problem because Amazon, as a company, has gotten their branding right.

Yes, even though there are still chances of people buying fake products on Amazon, the measures the company has put in place, help to curtail such occurrences. And if things like that happen, Amazon helps to protect the interest of the buyer by offering them refunds. All these and more are the things that have made Amazon become the trusted online giant that it is today.

Since Amazon is a well-known brand, reputable for its ability to protect the interest of the customer; if you pitch an Amazon product to your prospects, they would likely not have any objection regarding the authenticity of the products you are promoting. Also, your prospect knows that if they do not get the original product, they could simply return it and get a refund.

All this means that promoting Amazon products will be so easy for you. You don't have to say many words; you do not need to provide social proof or testimonials. You also do not need to do aggressive marketing. Simply put, Amazon's shiny brand image would simply rub off on you as an affiliate marketer, thus making things relatively easier for you.

Furthermore, millions, if not billions of transactions are carried out on Amazon every day. This means that the probability of getting someone to buy something through your affiliate link is quite high. All you need to do is to know the right products to promote, and the best ways to promote them and you are already on your way to making a living as an affiliate marketer.

2. It is easier

When compared to the other affiliate marketing networks or the other affiliate programs, Amazon affiliate marketing program could be likened to a walk in the park. To make it into so many other affiliate marketing programs, you would need to meet some requirements, and there are some restrictions too.

Many people just get into a buying mode when they visit the platform. So, if you know a good way of sending affiliate traffic to the site, your job is almost done by half. Once the traffic gets to the site, they would likely get into a buying mode, then go on a shopping spree, and you earn a commission.

3. There are billions of products to promote

As long as Amazon affiliate program is concerned, the sky is big enough for everybody as there are billions of products to promote and earn a commission. In addition to the already existing products, more are added on a daily basis. Furthermore, newer models of products, especially gadgets are introduced into the market every day, and they would find their way into Amazon.

So, there are always thousands of hot selling products to promote, and if one product starts recording low sales, you could easily research and find new hot selling products to promote. No matter the niche you choose, there will always be something on Amazon to promote.

4. You can make money from sales of products you didn't pitch

This is one of the greatest advantages of the Amazon affiliate program. You can make a lot of money selling products that you have not pitched. For instance, let's say your niche is audio equipment, and you do review all kinds of microphones and recommend them to people.

What happens is that if you refer someone to Amazon, and perhaps, the person gets to Amazon, changes their mind and decides to buy a TV set instead, as long as the purchase was made within 24 hours from the time you referred the customer to Amazon, you will still earn a commission even though the customer ended up buying another product instead of the one you recommended to them.

Remember, just like any other affiliate marketing program, Amazon gives you a unique affiliate link for each product you want to promote. It is this affiliate link that is used to track all the traffic that comes to the Amazon website through your efforts. Now, if a sale happens through your link, it is recorded in your name. Amazon uses what is called sticky cookies to make that possible.

The fact that you could earn money for products you did not pitch makes Amazon affiliate one of the best affiliate marketing programs. The reason is not hard to guess – all you need to make money is to send traffic to the Amazon website. If the customer you send to the site gets there and buys an entirely different item within 24 hours, then you still earn.

The commission you receive from Amazon for promoting their products ranges from 4% to 7% of the price of the product. Sometimes, high ticket items have bigger affiliate commissions while low ticket items have lower affiliate commissions, but this is not a written rule.

Which niche should I promote on Amazon?

When it comes to Amazon affiliate marketing, no niche can be said to be unprofitable. The reason for this is that you only need to push traffic to Amazon, and even the customer ends up buying another product, you still make money as long as the purchase happened within 24 hours.

Nevertheless, there are still some niches that attract the most traffic, and if you promote products in these niches, there are high chances that your audience would buy them. So, you still need to make sure that you are not just promoting any niche that comes to your mind.

That being said, the three evergreen niches still remain the best that you could promote on Amazon. However, when promoting products in such niches, you need to dig deeper or niche down until you arrive at a specialized sub-niche. The three most evergreen niches include health/wellness, money/wealth, and romance. You may find the games/hobbies niche to be a good one as well.

The health niche on Amazon, for instance, has a lot of interesting products which you could promote. Yes, people may not be able to buy drugs on Amazon, but there are thousands of health products they could buy and improve their health.

For instance, Apple iWatch helps people to measure their heart rate and perform a lot of other health checks. Even though the watch falls under gadgets, it could also fall under the health niche as well. So, if you want to promote the iWatch, you could promote it as an electronic gadget and a health product.

There are also thousands of similar health products on Amazon which you could promote and make money. Most of your audience have one health problem or the other, and they might have tried so many solutions to no avail. Now, if you help them point them to an Amazon product that could help their situation, they would likely buy the product and put some affiliate commissions in your pocket.

For instance, a lot of people suffer from back pain– and if you show such people that they could get relief from back pain by using an inversion therapy machine which could be gotten on Amazon, they would most likely want to try out the product, thus putting some affiliate commissions in your pocket.

The Amazon website has lots of products that help people to monitor their health or maintain a healthy lifestyle. These products are not hard to find – and if you promote them to those who really need them, then you can easily make money. Apart from health products, other products you could find in the health niche include eBooks that teach people how to live healthily and so on.

Just like the health niche, you could find good products in the money/wealth niches, romance niches, and the games/hobbies niches. All these are niches that are evergreen – people spend money on products in these niches. Some people don't even know that many of the products on Amazon exist – so, if you show such people that the products they need exist on Amazon, they would most likely buy and help you earn money in return.

In addition to the evergreen niches, which are unarguably the largest, there are still millions of other niches you could find products to promote. For instance, the gadgets niche is a great one for many reasons. Every other month, new electronic gadgets find their way into the market. However, people do not just go to the market to buy these products, they often wait for others to buy and give reviews.

If you show a prospective buyer of an electronic gadget the features of the gadget, you will help the potential buyer make an informed decision, and they could choose to buy through the link you provided. Mobile devices and other electronic devices are some of the hottest selling products on Amazon.

Remember, by describing some of the niches that sell well on Amazon; I am not by any means urging you to delve into those niches. Take the information you have received here to be for educational purposes only. You still need to do your own research and find out the type of Amazon products you would want to promote. When it comes to affiliate marketing and internet marketing as a whole, two people may have the same experience or knowledge and still get different results. So, it is important that you do your own research instead of relying on only the information you have been fed.

The best way to find great niches that do well on Amazon is to actually visit the website and see what people are willing to spend money on. If you are observant enough, you might find some good products to promote right on Amazon's homepage. On Amazon's homepage, they often list some of their best selling products.

When you visit the different categories, you will find bestsellers' list that contains the bestselling products in each category. Explore the products on the list and get an idea of the types of products that are doing well.

If you are new to the Amazon website and you do not know how to find the best selling products in any category, simply head to google, and type, "Amazon products bestseller's list." When you click on the first result on Google, you will be taken to the Amazon bestsellers' list. If you don't want to go through that lengthy process, simply click on this link (https://www.amazon.com/Best-Sellers/zgbs) and you will be taken to the bestsellers' list directly.

You will get a lot of ideas and even find some products and niches you never thought existed. So, the key to finding a good niche to promote on Amazon is research – don't depend on anyone to spoon feed you.

How to join Amazon affiliate program

Joining Amazon affiliate program is free – you simply need to visit Amazon affiliate program website and register. On the site, you will see a button that says, "Join Now For Free," click on it, fill out the registration form with your correct information and you are good to go.

If you already have a blog, then you would want to promote niches that are related to your blog. You could just promote the products to your blog audience and earn. However, if you do not have a blog already, you may need to develop a microblog or a niche blog which you will use for promoting your Amazon affiliate products.

How to extract your affiliate link

For you to earn money from the sales of an Amazon product as an affiliate, you need to extract an affiliate link for that product and use the link when you are making posts on your blog or sending marketing emails. Getting the affiliate link for a product could seem hard for a newbie; however, it is not all that complicated. Here are some of the steps you need to take to extract the affiliate link of any product on Amazon.

- Log in to your Amazon affiliate program account.
- Use the search bar to locate the product you want to promote. Simply type the names of the product you discovered in the bestsellers' list into the search bar. The products will pop up if they are among those that affiliates can promote.
- <u>Extract the links for the product. Repeat step two above for each of the products you want to promote.</u>

Let's go over the steps in detail

Once you log in to your Amazon affiliate marketing program account, look at the top menu, situated next to the "Home" button is a "product linking tab." Hover your mouse over this tab, and there will be a drop-down menu. Select the very first option that says, "Product link." Look further down the new page that opens, and you will see a search bar.

Next, enter the keyword for the product you want to promote. For instance, if you wish to promote training boots for men, simply type, "training boots" into the search bar and click "Go." If you know the exact name of the product, you could consider typing it directly into the search bar.

Once you hit the "Go" button, some search results related to the keywords or search terms you typed will be displayed. Located next to each search result, you will see an orange button that will provide the affiliate link for that specific product. Click on the arrow next to where it says, "Get link." When you click on that, you will receive a pop-up box containing the affiliate link to the product.

On close observation, you will notice that the link doesn't really look nice, and if you use the link as it is on your blog, it could be misconstrued as a spam link. How do you solve this puzzle? On top of the box that pops up, you will see two buttons. One says, "Copy and paste the link below," while the other says, "shorten link with amazon.to."

Now, click on the second button, and the affiliate link will be shortened to something more appealing and shorter. There are also other link shortening services that can serve a similar purpose, like bit.ly, etc. Now, include the link thus gotten in your product reviews, YouTube description boxes, social media posts, or any other place where you intend to be generating traffic for your affiliate products. Repeat this process for all the products you want to promote.

There are a lot of ways you can make money with Amazon, like selling items on the Amazon store or ebooks on Kindle and CreateSpace. However, one of the most interesting ways you can get started on Amazon is as an Amazon affiliate. These are a few reasons why being an Amazon affiliate is one of the best ways to make money on Amazon:

1) It is free to join

2) There are low startup costs

3) The business model is quite simple

It's completely free to join the Amazon Associates program. As long as you have a website, you can apply! If you don't have a website, not to worry, we will be covering the right type of website you need to help you generate the most money.

If you do not have a website, you can set one up on WordPress. It costs very little to have your website up and running in 5 minutes. Your total cost per month from a popular host such as Bluehost comes to about $20 a month and you require only very little knowledge of website design to tweak your website to suit your preference.

Being an Amazon affiliate is budget friendly as you don't stock or hold inventory, you are not required to buy goods, and you don't have to deal with any logistics such as shipping and delivery. The best part is that the process is fully automated.

Getting Started

There are a couple of steps you need to take to get started and be successful as an Amazon affiliate.

Build a Website: There are lots of online platforms that offer a one-click service. WordPress and Tumblr offer a ready-built framework for affiliate marketers. However, you will be required to acquire some knowledge on website design to help tweak your website for better functionality and great user experience.

Research Content: After designing your website, you need to create content that will bring in the users. Amazon encourages affiliates to create good content to help attract and give value to prospective customers. This will also help in avoiding the Google search hammer as Google prefers audience-focused, high-quality authority websites with helpful content as compared to niche sites.

What this means is that instead of making a low-quality niche website or a blog that is filled with a lot of product reviews, it is better to focus on building a high-quality authority website that is filled with solution oriented content.

There are also tools you can use to search for outranked keywords relevant to your topic. These tools will help to give you an insight into what content people are searching for so you can tailor your write-up to match the correct keywords. One free tool that is available to you is the Google search bar.

The Google search bar has a feature called Google Instant. This feature is what seems to want to help you finish your sentence when typing into the search bar. These suggestions that Google offers should definitely be used in choosing the right topics.

Write Beautiful Articles: Writing is pretty easy. You don't have to be a great writer or word Smith to produce good articles. Most people visiting your website come to your website to be educated, entertained or inspired. Your writing doesn't have to be formal, it can even be casual. Sometimes, you will see that casual writing will outperform formal writing. It doesn't take a genius to write great content and most people are only searching for your experience on the subject matter. So write freely!

Link to Products: Find the product you want to promote on Amazon, you will find a picture and link to the product. It is this link that you put on your articles that are promoting products on your website. You need learn the art of placing links in articles and ensure that they are not out of place while still using relevant hyperlinks.

How Money is Made

If someone follows your recommendation and clicks on your link, they are taken to the Amazon product's page. You get credit for any purchases made within 24 hours. If the customers place some items in their cart, you will get a credit if they purchase those items within 90 days.

You will earn a 4% commission for any sale at the start but if you make more sales, they can raise the commission to 10%. Depending on the number of people who make sales through your affiliate link, you can earn a lot of money. This is the reason why you should continuously be looking for new ways to promote your website.

Chapter 5. Start Promoting Products

I believe by now you understand that affiliate marketing is all about promoting a product. Thus, earning from it depends on how you properly promote products on your website.

Certainly, it requires efforts and strategies to start converting affiliate links into sales. Your website must be a guiding tool for online users who are looking for products to satisfy their needs.

The real sense of affiliate marketing is not selling a product on your website but rather promoting products to get a successful buying decision. You'll be using your website to create quality content that promotes Amazon products.

a. How to Promote Amazon Products Effectively

First, be familiar with the important rules in promoting products online particularly with Amazon affiliate links.

1. Get active with your blog.

Your website will be the 'bread and butter' of your online business, so it requires valuable information for your visitors. Having regular quality contents on your website is a very good search engine optimization strategy. Google is able to see that your website is active with your added contents on a regular basis.

To maintain your affiliate marketing business, your blog must not be overly focused on a single product, otherwise, people will only know your site to be biased and out for money. If you promote too many products in a short period of time without providing other valuable information, you'll end up with no loyal followers.

Loyalty and trust from visitors need to be established beforehand. It becomes easier to get people and buy a product that you recommend if they trust you enough with what you're saying on your blog.

Getting active with your blog is the key to win people's trust. Practically, overkilling your content with affiliate links is a big NO!

2. Keep relevant products.

Look for products that focus on your niche market. Your affiliate links must be relevant products only. Think of products which are closely related to your niche.

Find products that can be useful to your niche and promote exactly how it was useful to you which brought you to recommend it to others.

3. Write interesting and honest reviews.

The best way to promote and make money with Amazon is to talk about your experience with certain products. Create in-depth reviews for your visitors.

Be honest when you write product reviews. The best way to give an honest review is to try the product. You may also ask someone else to try it for you. In doing so, you can be sure of the quality of the products you're promoting.

Write your review as simple as telling them your experience with the product. Mention some key facts like how you came across with the product, what are the features that delighted you most, and why others love it too.

You may also include the product's price and how you compare it to other products. But there is a rule to maintain a balance of the product's pros and cons, so you may not sound like over promoting a product on your blog.

To make your content more interesting, write some buying tips and advice. Definitely, it makes sense to your readers.

Keep writing contents for people in a "buying mood." In the long run, your visitors will look at you as an expert in your small niche.

On the other hand, if you're just selling affiliate products on your blog, without giving valuable information to your readers, you won't generate sales from it. People visiting your blog will feel when you're only making some stories out of nowhere.

Make your content interesting and more visitors will get hooked with your posts.

4. Build affiliate links on your blog regularly.

It is advisable not to put many affiliate links in the first paragraph of your review or better have your first affiliate link in the second paragraph.

Here's what you can do. Use at least two links per post. Take note that a link to the end of your review has greater tendency to convert a sale when a visitor clicks your link after reading your review.

It is important that you keep note that Amazon links must have a no-follow attributes (use rel="nofollow") to avoid being penalized by Google.

Here's a simple guide on how to put Amazon affiliate link in your content.

- *Log in to your Amazon account*

- *Find a product and look for the link "link to this page" text*

- *There will be 3 choices of links: (1) text and image (2) text only (3) image only*

- *Highlight the HTML code and copy it*

- *Go to your post and paste the code*

Choosing which type of link to use depends on your preference and which will work best for your target market.

There is a tool to track your links when you create multiple affiliate tags. Initially, using different tags can help you compare any type of link and see which type of link generates sales on your blog.

Comparing each type of links, most people are drawn to buy a product if they see an image of the product. On the other hand, banner ads may be least effective for some to generate sales. Among the types of link, using a text link within the post is the common option to put affiliate links. It's preferable that when using a text link, edit the link text to avoid a long product title. Use a shortened text with two or three words for the product name.

Looking for a convenient way to build links on your website?

Try the WordPress plugin called Easy Azon. It makes it easy to add links. With the plugin, it enables searching and adding products from your WordPress Dashboard easily. It saves your time just by getting the product information and images for you.

Watch this YouTube video tutorial to help you start building affiliate links to promote Amazon products on your website.

YouTube Tutorial:

- How to Insert Amazon Affiliate Links into your Blog Posts.

5. Proper article keywords are important.

Maintaining an active blog is not enough to keep promoting products on your website. Keyword strategy must be done properly to have your content be optimized for the search engine. Having a high search ranking creates more chance of people seeing your website.

Now, the efforts you started in finding your niche plays a big role in promoting products. Writing your post requires proper article keywords to get traffic.

And so, keyword research is necessary whenever you write content. Keywords should resemble the vocabulary of your target market. You need to think how your target market would think to identify keywords they will use in searching the web.

Just Google your proposed focus keyword and compare your article with the first two result pages if it has same keywords on their titles. You may also look into the pages to decide on possible content ideas that may inspire you to include onto your blog.

Picking a focus keyword for your article is not easy. Take advantage of some tools that make your online business a bit easier. I have listed here the most useful tools in finding proper keywords namely:

- *GOOGLE ADWORDS KEYWORD PLANNER- A tool that enables you to find new and related keywords without considering the search volume data. It helps you come up with potential keyword ideas. This is the same tool that is used in finding your niche.*

- *YOAST SUGGESTS - A tool that gives a quick find of long tail keywords that uses the Google Suggest functionality. It enables keyword expansions from what Google suggests.*

- *GOOGLE TRENDS - A tool that compares traffic of different sets of keywords, which also includes a comparison of various geographical regions.*

Aside from these tools, make use also of your internal search engine. Results of keywords that your actual visitors key in from your website that didn't get any results should be included on your keyword list. You may check the results of those keywords from Google Analytics, a WordPress plugin.

Doing keyword research will provide you list of relevant keywords that can help you better promote products on your website with the perfect keyword.

b. Blogging Tips to Maximize Your Sales

This is the stage that you will "plant, water, and nurture" your website, so your online business will bear fruits. It matters that you know and follow the rules in promoting products on your website.

Promoting products doesn't end with following the rules. The most difficult yet fulfilling part of promoting products on your blog is to make visitors feel the convenience when they visit your website. It's like a one-stop shop where everything they need will be answered just by reading your posts.

You'll be fulfilled when your website gets promoted through word of mouth or reviews of people who visited your blog. They can't help but share their great experience upon visiting your website. Your product should be as good as your content to create a perfect experience for your visitors that eventually translates to income.

To help you promote your blog and products you recommend, your creativity is a big plus in getting the right set of products for your blog. It may be a tough job to showcase the most appropriate products for your niche market. And so, I have listed some content suggestions that you may include on your website to maximize sales from referred Amazon links.

1. List popular products.

Your visitors will find it convenient to see some lists of products that you recommend. Do this on a monthly or quarterly basis. Though you will be focusing on your niche, this can be an opportunity to introduce some related products or new topics. In this way, you can show your visitors how you value them by providing lists of popular products.

2. Offer seasonal content.

Your target market is expecting products from time to time especially on special occasions. Get this opportunity to post your recommended products for the season with the Amazon links.

The most awaited seasons are Christmas, Thanksgiving, Valentine's Day, and Halloween. You can research on other occasions of other countries if you want to target specific regions for a particular season.

3. Show the bestseller products.

People are interested to know the products that most people buy. They tend to buy products that most people are buying. It's a human nature to follow and trust the majority, isn't it? Also, recommending the bestseller products on your blog is easier to promote because it's proven to be a saleable item.

4. Get promotional products with special offers or discounts.

Keep yourself updated with Amazon's special promotions that are related to your niche because it is a worthwhile content on your website. You may note on your post the discount it offers to catch the eye of your readers.

5. Encourage reader's reviews and comments.

When a reader sees other readers recommending the same as what your content is saying on your blog, your intent becomes more genuine. There is a tendency that more readers will be interested in trying the product. This strategy will also show how you value their opinions and can be a start of a conversation with your readers.

The sales you'll generate from affiliate links promoted on your blog will primarily come from converted loyalty and trust readership. Trust develops once your readers get connected with your blog on a regular basis. Remember that it takes readers to trust you enough to consider your recommendations on your blog. So, you have to ensure that your website contents are intended to build trust.

Your online business doesn't end with setting up your website, writing reviews, and putting affiliate links and widgets to promote Amazon products on your website. It requires more time and effort to be consistent and get the highest profit from it. Strategy to get traffic for your online business is another effort to make.

From the beginning of finding your niche to writing articles on your website, keywords you use must be well researched to gain traffic. In online business, traffic is considered an effective but difficult way to promote a product.

All internet marketers, who wish to make it big, compete for traffic on the web. And so, you must be ready to compete as well.

Getting traffic means getting exposure. No matter how well designed your blog is and how well thought your product reviews are, it will never reach your audience if you don't have traffic.

You'll need to learn some strategies to increase traffic, so online users will land on your pages and discover what your website has in store for them.

Here are some easy ways to start get traffic, be exposed and popular with your blog:

- *Let your friends, families and acquaintances know about your blog*

- *Use your email to put your website link as part of your signature*

- *Create some video and leave a link at YouTube*

- *Be active in social media*

I'd like to stress the importance of social media on your online business. Use your social media account to target a specific audience. You should post attention grabber headlines to promote your blog or introduce a recommended product.

Definitely, your social media accounts will play an essential role in promoting Amazon products. This is the reason why in building your website, it is advisable to create a social media account.

Getting traffic, being exposed and popular with your blog is not only promoting a recommended Amazon product to your visitors but also getting people in the door of Amazon in a relevant way.

Isn't it cool that you still get a commission from the purchases of referred visitors to Amazon even if it is not the product you promoted?

I'm sure that promoting products on your website will get more fun when you get to know more of your readers. More ideas will surely come your way.

Just keep in mind the product selection and blogging tips I shared with you so you can maximize your earning. These tips will ease any difficulty in maintaining your online business.

Chapter 6. Attracting Traffic And SEO

I'm a big believer in free traffic. Believe it or not, even though it's 2019, SEO is still relevant and it's very possible to drive free traffic to your website. The key is knowing how to do it the right way. Google is constantly changing rules but one rule that never changes is that Google is going to favor and authority site over any other type of website. And the authority site is basically one that provides useful content to viewers.

Don't Duplicate Content

You should also have some awareness of what Google doesn't like. One thing it doesn't like it is duplicate content. If you put duplicate content on your website, you're going to penalize it. In fact, it might even cause them to host your website. So, rule number one you should apply doesn't matter what it is to write your own content. If you're not up to the task to do this, then go on a site like a fiver, and hire people to do it for you. It's better to do that then it is to post duplicate content. But the best possible way to go about this is to actually write your own content.

Avoid Keyword Stuffing

Rule number two is don't do keyword stuffing. Using the right keywords is going to be a big part of your strategy for attracting traffic to your website. But if you engage in keyword stuffing that's going to backfire. You want to use your keywords as a part of natural writing. Google can tell if there is keyword stuffing. And guess what, they have a lot of experience finding it out and detecting it. So, there is no way that you going to get past them and use keyword stuffing to your advantage.

Natural backlink patterns from social media

Rule number three is the post in a natural fashion. You should start off the site by posting a lot of content but then make it look natural after that, post about once per day. You also want to make your backlink pattern look natural. That is one reason why you should have a Facebook account and a Facebook page that is directly tied to your blog. Google looks for natural trying to spread the word by posting on social media. So, you can begin by posting on the Facebook page. Twitter isn't as effective however I would still create a Twitter account for your niche and use it for the purpose of backlinking to the main website. So, every time that you write a blog post, go ahead and posted on Twitter. The Google search robots are going to note that you are doing this and by making it look natural it's going to give your website more weight.

There're other social media sites that you can use to generate backlinks. Consider using Pinterest and Tumblr. There also used to be a good site for bringing traffic called Stumble Upon, but I believe it's under a different name now and doesn't get the traffic it used to.

Write Articles Suitable for Your Niche

The title of the section is actually a little bit misleading. Obviously, you're going to be writing content on your blog that is relevant to the niche. I actually mean something different by this, so what's explain. What you want to do first is go to Google keyword planner and build up a large list of long tail keywords for your niche. Hopefully, they are relevant ones and if you don't find enough long tail keywords you can always turn the main keyword into a long tail keyword by appending a certain phrase or word to it. Let's take an example.

Let's say that you're selling Apple computers as an affiliate. The word MacBook is the main keyword. When you have a main keyword like that the competition is so fierce and That in 2019 it's probably not very possible for a new website to get ranked for the keyword in any reasonable amount of time. That doesn't mean you don't use the keyword in your articles, but it shouldn't be the focus of an article.

However, we could turn it into a niche keyword. So, for example, the niche phrase or long tail keyword could be using a MacBook for video processing. So, this is the phrase that you want to use in your title, and then you're going to want to put it in your article about three times. Remember don't overdo it. The Google robots are going to recognize it if you put using a MacBook for video processing in your article 10 times.

However, I said to write an article suitable for a niche. So, what does that mean?

Go to Google and then search on the keyword. Then you want to analyze articles that come up on the first page. Be sure to ignore any articles that are paid advertisements. Only use articles that are organic to do your analysis.

The first thing that you should look for is to determine how long the articles are the people are writing that is getting them on the front page. The second thing you want to look for is whether your search term is on their page. If so, count the number of times it shows up.

Do this for all the articles on page 1 of Google search. Then take the average of the count. Do this both for the lengths of the articles and also for the count of the keyword phrase. You will also want to note any differences between articles that show up at the very top and articles that are at the bottom.

When you have this data, then you have a guideline for the best way to write your article. So, if it turns out that the keyword phrase appears five times on average for page-one articles, then you know that that's about how many times you should use the phrase in your article. Also if it turns out that the articles say on average 750 words, then you should make yours about that size as well. I would make mine a little bit longer so I would aim for maybe 850 words.

Use Images and Sections to Break up Articles

Besides keywords, Google also looks at the quality of the articles on websites. So, one of the things you want to do just to make sure to break up your article into different sections, using heading text to separate the sections. The Google robots are going to be looking for the headline tags when they call your page. So, you want reasonably divided sections. What you don't want is to have one long stream of text. That is definitely going to hurt your search rankings.

The next thing you're going to want to do is to include some images and even better if you can link to videos in your articles. The search engine robots are also looking to see how interesting and visually appealing pages. Now they are actually trying to see the page as in seeing it with your own eyes. But they check for visual appeal by noting whether or not the text is broken up by other types of media. The reason that they do this is that people find images visually appealing and human beings are visual creatures. So, it helps to make your website more valuable. People also like video content and so you want some video content as well. Every single article you write doesn't have to have video content but you should be trying to put some on your website. And also never skimp on the written content because when it comes down to it, that's the king.

Using Content to Drive Traffic

Alright, so what we want to do this fall that process for each keyword that we choose to write an article about. And you're going to be wanting to write substantial articles several times a week.

Yes, I know it sounds like a lot of work but over time this can translate into actual money.

So, the key is to target multiple keywords and most of them should be the long tail types that we've been talking about. Of course, you should also target some of the bigger keywords as well. But you want to keep building out your website so that it ends up with a very large number of pages over time.

So, to get a head start that's why I suggest an initial page count of 20. So, before you even create your blog, you're going to want to do a little bit of research on some long tail keywords so that you can put up to 20 articles relatively quickly once the blogs up and running.

So, besides a lot of content, the search engines also like to see that the website is active and relevant. So, they're also looking to see the content is being posted on a regular basis. It's probably not going to be necessary to be posting every single day the rest of your life after you get to level traffic that you like then maybe you can taper off a little bit.

It's going to be hard to actually spend time writing about a topic that you're not interested in. So obviously that's not something that you really want to do. That means selecting your product, in the beginning, is a very important step.

Finding Target Clients

If you structure your website in the way that I've been describing, funding target clients is something that's going to come naturally. You want to be focusing mainly on writing content that they are really interested in. After Google starts indexing your site, and articles you write start moving up in the search page rankings, you are naturally going to be attracting the right target clients. You have to give this some time to work, however, but the more content that you write in a shorter time period, along with utilizing social media sites such as YouTube, Facebook, Twitter, Pinterest, and Instagram, the faster this procedure is going to go along.

Types of Articles to Write

Now you definitely should be using a process of using the long tail keywords to guide your choice of a lot of topics for your articles. However, I'm going to give you some tips on some specialized articles that you should include along with the other ones.

The first of these is going to be a compare and contrast article. So, what you want to do did you want to sign up as an affiliate for two different products in the same niche. It turns out that a lot of people are going to be already looking for the title of the article that you're going to write.

So just to use cars as an example although I'm not sure you can sell cars as an affiliate, you could write an article titled "Toyota Corolla versus Honda civic, which car is better."

Then in your article, you simply describe the features of each and your opinions about the features, and then at the end of the article maybe you recommend one or the other. Either way, throughout the article you should include buttons that maybe say "get more information here" or something like that. The buttons within be linked directly to the sales page of the product. And you should definitely link to both products in the article. This is a great strategy because it allows you to profit from both affiliate products. Some people are going to like one or the other, but it doesn't matter to you which one they like, because if you set this up right, then you're going to be an affiliate for both.

Another type of article that you can write which will be very helpful for this process of driving your site, is to make top 10 lists. You have probably already noticed many people join us on their blogs already. It's a very easy way to write an article without having to put much thought into the topic. If you are an affiliate for a site like Amazon, using our previous example of drones, you could be an affiliate for 10 different drones that are for sale. So, you could write an article titled "The top 10 drones of 2019". For each drone, you could have a paragraph or so reviewing it, and then, of course, you would include your affiliate link that takes them to Amazon to purchase is a drone.

You can even do this for click bank products. So, you could write the same type of article for click bank products as well. You just review each of them and then put a link at the bottom of the review pointing back to their sales page.

Another type of article to include on your blog is a long personal review of a single product that you've written and personally tried it out. This can be a very effective type of article, and articles written in this fashion often come up high in Google rankings.

Chapter 7. Optimize These On-Page Elements

Nevertheless, because of its importance to the organic traffic your niche site generates, you should not overlook it.

In this subsection, we shall cover important On-page elements you should optimize to improve your chances of ranking first on SERP for your keywords:

1: Title Tag

The title tag (or just the title) of your pages and content is the first on-page element you should optimize. The general optimization ideas here it to ensure that in addition to being short and descriptive, the title of a page or content does a thorough job of letting audiences and search bots know the nature of a page, i.e. the topic covered within content or a page.

Worth remembering is that the title tag is the first thing crawlers look at and index. As such, you should optimize it accordingly.

Backlinko, an authority site on all things SEO and online marketing, suggests starting your title with a keyword. When doing so is impossible or an instance where doing so compromises readability, optimize the title with users in mind and only insert keywords where it feels natural. Nevertheless, for the best SEO juice, start your titles with keywords.

In addition to starting your title with keywords, also add modifiers such as "year," "best," review," "guide," etc. Adding modifiers to your title improves your SEO and helps you rank better for search terms that have the said modifier. You should also wrap your title in a <h1> tag. You can do this manually but since we are using WordPress to manage our niche sites, the process is automatic.

In addition to the above, another way to optimize your title tag is to add various elements such as your site and business name. Ensuring the title tag has your site and business name is an effective branding strategy. When you have a strong brand that potential targets type into a search bar, including your brand name in the title will make your brand name indexable, which will make the site more accessible to users.

Seeing that the title is an important on-page ranking factor, when you want to rank for specific keywords, ensure you use keywords within the title. When you do so, Google immediately recognizes the nature/topic of your niche site. When keywords naturally appear on the title tag and within your content, Google will feel inclined to give you first position or first page ranking for the keywords you are targeting. Even as you optimize your title and content with keywords, keep in mind keyword stuffing and aim to avoid it as much as possible.

2: Meta Tags

Today, Meta descriptions do not carry as much SEO weight as they once did. Nevertheless, optimizing it is a good SEO practice since the Meta description appears on SERP and search spiders still crawl it.

Keep your Meta description short, keyword rich, and ensure it describes the nature of a page or piece of content. Think of the Meta description as a chance to optimize a page for search spiders while at the same time informing potential audiences that land on SERP why they should navigate to your page instead of navigating to any other page Google returns for specific keywords. If your Meta description does a good job of describing what an audience will get from reading a page, you are likely to attract a visit from that audience. Aim to ensure your Meta description is not generic. Write it well [with the end user in mind] and optimize it with keywords.

You can make the Meta description as long as you want. However, the search engine results page only displays 160 characters and truncates the rest. Because of this, aim to ensure that the first 160 characters contain your intended keywords and worded in a way that attracts clicks.

More importantly, avoid using double quotation marks in the Meta description. Whenever you use double quotations, Google will truncate the description from the point you insert the quotation marks. When creating your Meta descriptions, avoid using all non-alphanumeric characters.

Head to the resources below to supplement the Meta description knowledge you have learned:

https://moz.com/learn/seo/meta-description

https://yoast.com/meta-descriptions/

3: HTML Tags

How you use keywords to optimize your content for search is very important to your ranking. As you create content, you will notice the need to segment your content either as a way to make it easier to navigate or to emphasize specific areas. When such a need arises, you will use HTML tags. When using HTML tags to optimize your content for SEO, we normally use the tags: <h1>, <h2>, <h3>, <h4>, and <h5> tags.

When you use HTML tags, the text within the tags changes depending on the tag used; for instance, it can change to bold or italic. For SEO purposes, the <h1> tag has the most SEO juice and you should use it only once on your title and nowhere else within the content lest you confuse search spiders. To segment your content, use the tag <h2> through to <h5>.

To improve your SEO, optimize these tags with lookalike keywords. In addition to allowing you to optimize your content with similar keywords thereby allowing you to tell search spiders the nature of your content, using HTML tags is also good practice since segmenting your content makes navigation easier, which makes your content and niche site more user friendly.

While we are still talking about making content appealing, you should note that using text styles gives you a chance to emphasize specific elements of your content. For instance, emboldening text gives Google spiders the impression that the emboldened text is important. Part of the reason for this is because when you specify special text styles such as bold and italic, it encloses the text in HTML tag.

At this point in your affiliate marketing business and optimizing it for SEO, pay attention to the title tag, the Meta description, and the <h1>-<h5> tags.

The following resource from industry leader Kissmetrics has more information on HTML tags:

https://blog.kissmetrics.com/website-source-code-seo/

4: Keywords Optimization

Although, "keyword stuffing," is something you should avoid at all cost, keywords remain a fundamental part of search and SE and as such, no well-informed webmaster can overlook the need to optimize his or her niche site with the keywords he or she intends to rank for and attract customers. Optimizing your niche site with keywords is an on-page SEO undertaking.

As you optimize your niche site, aim to use a healthy amount of keywords so that in addition to your site being user friendly, it also becomes easier for search spiders to recognize the nature of your site and relate it to user queries.

At this point in the development of search algorithms, Google and other search engines have the ability to decipher keyword intent. Because of this development, where you use your keywords, an element called keyword placement, does not matter as much as it used to in the early days of search.

The easiest way to optimize your pages and site in general with keywords is to create your pages and all content with the end user in mind. Essentially, if placing keywords within your pages or content compromises readability, avoid doing so. Only use keywords where it feels natural and where it does not compromise readability. The more you concentrate on being helpful to your readers, the easier it will be to balance and have a healthy sprinkle of keywords within your pages and content.

When using WordPress as your content management system, you do not have to concern yourself with elements such as Keyword density. Installing a SEO plugin such as Yoast SEO will guide you and help you strike the perfect keyword density balance.

If you would like to couple the plugin with general knowledge, keep the following in mind: moderately sprinkle your keywords within the page or content all without compromising readability and the quality of the content. As you write and publish more content for your niche site, you will learn more about what works for you and your audiences.

As you infuse keywords {naturally} into your content and pages, also aim to use a healthy sprinkle of related keywords and synonyms. For instance, if a keyword phrase you are targeting has a synonym, you can use the alternative keyword/s within your content or if need be, use the keyword/s to optimize your <h2> to <h5> title tags. The use of alternative keywords allows you to optimize your content with keywords all without keyword stuffing tactics of pushing your keyword density too high.

Another effective way to optimize your content with keywords is to optimize it using long tail keywords. Compared to short tail or head tail keywords, it is easier to rank for longer search terms aka long tail keywords. Throughout the keyword research process, you should have come up with a healthy mix of head tail and long tail keywords you can use to optimize individual pages or pieces of content.

5: Internal Link Optimization

Anchor texts, the visible, clickable text in a hyperlink, are another SEO signal that Google uses to determine the nature of a page or content. As you optimize your niche site with the aim of attracting as much organic traffic as you can, also optimize internal and outbound links with related keywords. Doing this improves your search rankings. Content management systems such as WordPress enclose hyperlinks in the (<a>) tag. Because of their enclosure in a tag, Google and other search spiders tend to pay special attention to anchor text, which is why you should optimize them with keywords.

As you optimize internal and external links with organic traffic and search engine optimization in mind, adhere to the following:

First, your anchor texts should have a healthy serving of keywords or related keywords. Adding keywords to your anchor text gives outbound and internal links context and meaning, which makes it easier for search engines to relate your content to that on the page you have linked to on another website or another area of your niche site.

Creating a proper internal linking structure is another important SEO element that in addition to improving user experience (great UX) will also improve your search engine ranking. Think of it this way.

6: Visual Optimization

Visual optimization is another important on-page optimization factor. When we say visual optimization, we mean you should optimize your content and pages by lacing it with all manners of multimedia.

According to Hubspot, when we hear something, we are probably going to remember only 10% of that information three days later. However, if we pair a relevant image with that same information, we retain about 65% of the information three days later. In addition, Hubspot found out that in 2017 and beyond, 43% of all consumers want to see more video.

Overlooking using multimedia to optimize your content and pages—and the subsequent use of keywords to optimize the images and vides you use—will negatively affect your SEO as well as your user experience.

As you use multimedia—images, videos, infographics, audio, etc.—to optimize your content and pages, optimize these elements using keywords because while Google spiders may be unable to read and index multimedia, they have the ability to read the titles and tags attached to the multimedia. *In the future, thanks to* Google's Cloud Vision API, *Google will be able to detect objects in images.*

Because at this point, search engine spiders can only read text, to enhance your ranking, optimize the multimedia you use within your pages and content with your main keywords as well as their alternatives. To do so, you will have to use the following special tags:

The alt text or alternate text describes your image to anyone that hovers a computer mouse over a piece of image used within your content or page. Because optimizing your multimedia with the alt text improves your SEO strategy, ensure that the text you use within the alt text is relevant to your content or page and is keyword rich—the alt text is an especially ideal place to use head tail keywords.

The name you give the multimedia files you use within your content and pages should be meaningful and related to the content and keywords you aim to optimize your content or page for. As an example, instead of using a filename such as DSC200566.jpg, you should change the file name to something related to the nature of the content of the page.

7: Mobile Friendliness

While it has not always been the case, today, mobile friendliness is a critical ranking factor and Google is on record stating that for searches conducted on mobile devices, it favors mobile friendly websites. Google indicates that about 60% of all searches are on mobile (smartphones).

What does this mean for you as an online business entrepreneur? It means that since most searches are mobile-based, you cannot afford to overlook optimizing your affiliate marketing business for mobile search. Doing so is especially important because Google clearly states that they have two indexes: a mobile and desktop index, and for mobile searches, favors mobile friendly sites over those that lack the same capability.

In 2018 and beyond, making your niche site responsive—meaning it can adopt to fit different devices—and mobile friendly is especially important because more than 50% of all internet users access the internet from their mobile devices.

Now that you have created your niche site and done a great job of furnishing it with keyword optimized content, you can use the Google mobile-friendly test tool to determine if your site is as mobile friendly as it can be:

https://www.google.com/webmasters/tools/mobile-friendly/

Determined to live up to its mission statement and purpose, and in a bid to give their users the fastest search experience and results, Google now shows accelerated mobile pages (AMP). AMP allows articles to load instantly with the main identification of such pages being a lightning bolt symbol.

The faster a page loads, the higher the likelihood that users will stay longer. Longer stay times influences bounce rates as well as conversion rates since when a user stays longer on a page, it gives you a chance to convince that audience and turn him or her into a lead, then a buying customer, and then a loyal, repeat customer. *AMP also has implications on your search engine ranking.*

Google's Mobile-friendly test tool is so effective that once you check your site for mobile friendliness, it displays the mobile friendliness of the site and in a case where the site is not mobile friendly, it displays the various changes and tweaks you need to make to ensure your site is mobile friendly.

Optimizing the above seven on-page optimization areas/factors will help how Google indexes your site; if you ace these 7 factors, your pages, content, and niche site should easily climb to the top of SERP for your intended keywords.

In addition to the above, you should also take note of something called technical SEO, aspects of SEO that are overly technical and thus require a bit of technical knowledge. Technical SEO involves elements such as site speed, structured data and schema, site architecture, and error pages and redirects.

While these on-page off-page elements are not as important as the ones we have discussed above and will discuss below in off-page SEO, they also affect how Google Crawlers and your audiences view your site and therefore, you should optimize for them too.

Action Step

In this chapter, we have discussed a number of on-page SEO factors that when optimized, will ensure your pages and content rank well for the keywords you are targeting. Take what you have learned here and implement it to your content as well as pages keeping in mind that this process works well when done in tandem with the creation of pages and content.

Back links are another important factor that Google uses to determine the relevance of a page as well as where to rank it on their index for specific search terms. Back linking is under off-page SEO, the opposite of on-page SEO.

Chapter 8. How To Do Affiliate Marketing Through Facebook

While most people head right to their blog when it is time to work with affiliate marketing, there are other ways that you can reach more people and earn money off your links. And the method we are going to look at now is affiliate marketing through Facebook.

Facebook is one of the biggest social media platforms out there with billions of profiles and people using this site each day around the world. This means that you get the benefit of potentially reaching a ton of people with your links, as long as you make sure you are doing it in the right way.

Before we get started with using Facebook on your affiliate links, you first need to set up the profile that you want to use. You can choose to work with your own personal profile, or you can choose to work with a business profile based on how you want to conduct your business. Make sure that it starts to show your brand and you only post things on the page, especially if it is your personal page, that lines up with the new brand and company that you are trying to work on.

Direct Facebook Traffic Over to Your Affiliate Page

Since most people already have their own Facebook accounts and know how to deal with opening up another one, it is time to move straight to the dirty work. You are able to use your Facebook audience in order to accumulate engaging likes until you have a ton of fans. But when you are working as an affiliate marketer, this isn't going to help you out until you are able to get some more of that traffic to head to your marketing page, so they make a purchase.

A good way to think about this is as a type of flirting that will help you to build up the relationships that you want, rather than going through with your guns blazing and sending out a lot of spam. Think of it this way, would you rather help out or look at a link from a close friend who showed the products, and actually talked to you on occasion without trying to sell you? Or would you rather have your inbox and page filled up with spam and messages about the product all the time? Your potential customer is going to feel the same way.

A good ratio for you to go with is about 80 percent entertaining content that has nothing to do with the selling (or at least a tiny amount of selling hidden in there), and 20 percent promotion. This ensures that you build up a good relationship with your potential customer without annoying them and putting them off from even looking at your page.

For Facebook advertising to work for your affiliate marketing, you need to make your potential customer genuinely like your page, using that 80 percent relevant and entertaining media. That way, when you do post some targeted promotions, they are more likely to at least take a look at it and maybe even consider purchasing the item.

What you should consider here is making sure that the thing you promote is the actual affiliate site rather than doing a direct sale. It is much better to turn the traffic into some new leads who are already familiar with the website that you are presenting, rather than trying to get more people interested in going to see your content, whether that is a blog post, or some special deal for them.

Once you are able to snag some new audience using an enticing reason for them to head back to your site, especially those who have been to the site in the first place, you can then send them back to the main affiliate or landing page, and even get them on your email list. This one thing is going to help you expand out the strategy that you have for affiliate marketing from just Facebook and your normal affiliate site. And if you are able to build up the email list that you have, you will really have some valuable customers who are highly likely to purchase from you in the future.

Facebook Advertising

Another option that you can work with is to not just focus on the people who are already on your page or profile but also work to get a portion of the very large audience base that is present on Facebook and get them sent over to your affiliate site. Facebook Ads is one of the best ways for you to do this. There are some different options that you can work with when you want to bring in Facebook Ads including pay per click advertising or paying per 1000 impressions. You can experiment with these to figure out which one is going to work the best for your needs.

Facebook Ads will help you to target the right audience for you because Facebook has information that can make your campaigns better. You can look up information about the age of users, their locations, where they work, what their interests are, and more. This can be great because you can highly target the audience you want to work with, and it pulls in traffic to one of your affiliates offers faster than before.

Setting up an ad on Facebook is pretty simple. You can go on your personal account or your business account and do the drop-down menu on the settings or from the small wheel that is right at the top right-hand side of the page. You should be able to see a lot of options on there that are meant to suit a wide variety of goals. If you want to make sure that more people see your page and can interact with it and engage, then you would go with the top option. Or for page Likes, you would select that option. To send these customers or audience members to your affiliate page you may want to try website conversions to help you track how many clicks are occurring and then converting to sign-ups for your email according to the plan.

If you want to use this campaign to get people to your offers or your content, you can try Clicks on Website. You can then go through and add in your website and some images to go with it. You should have more than one image in place here to really entice your customer base, but six is the amount that you should aim for and try to stick with the recommended size of an image that is about 600 by 315 pixels.

The next thing that you can work with is linking this new ad over to the Facebook page. The link will still make your customers go to your website when they click on it, but doing this option will make it easier to gain some more publicity in the process, and it builds up some links and associations between your site and your Facebook page. You can also work with adding in a call to action button to make things easier.

Chapter 9. How To Do Affiliate Marketing With Instagram

Instagram is one of the most popular platforms for social media out there. It doesn't matter what niche you want to go with, business, money, beauty, blogging, and food, everyone is on Instagram, and the pictures and method of working with the platform can make it really a popular platform to use.

There are a number of techniques that you can use in order to use Instagram to help with affiliate marketing. Instagram is sometimes a tricky platform for you to monetize with affiliate marketing, and you may want to work with some of the other opportunities that are out there first and gain some more experience. One of the issues can come from not being able to add in clickable links like you can with other social media platforms. But there are a few different ways that you can maximize the results that you get with Instagram, even as an affiliate marketer, including:

Add in the Affiliate Links to the Bio

You are only allowed to put one link into the bio that you write for Instagram, so you need to make sure that it really counts. Instead of linking back to an affiliate product, website, or blog post, using one link that will point back to a number of links instead. Some of the cool ways that you are able to do this include:

1. Linktree: This is a tool that is easy to set up and free to use. You can work with the premium option if you need it, but most people are going to be happy with the free account because it can do plenty. Linktree is going to provide you with a short link that you can then place into your bio, which can then display your list of links to any follower to click if they would like.

2. Create a menu page on the website: If you don't want to work with a third-party tool, you can also go through and create a page on your website. You can simply create a new page on your website and list out all the links that you want to work with. You can choose text images, or buttons to do this. On places like WordPress.com, you can use the Elementor to build up a really stunning page.

Include Some Affiliate Links in the Stories that You Do

Once you get to the 10,000-follower mark on Instagram, you will then gain the ability to add these kinds of links with your stories using the swipe up feature. When your follower looks at your story and then swipes up with that story, they will be following the link automatically right to the service or product page.

Of course, if you don't have these many followers, you won't be able to use this swipe up function on your pages. However, there are a few other things that you can choose to work with. You can include a shortened and easy to remember link to the story by working with bitly or Pretty Links. Some people choose to work with sharing links with the followers by reminding the story watchers to click back on the bio.

Some people decide to take the extra steps to make their account verified. Once your account is verified by Instagram, you will then be able to have the swipe up feature, regardless of how many people follow you. Verifying your account doesn't have to be difficult. You just need to go to Settings and then look for the option to Request Verification, and then follow the steps that are listed. You will need to submit a relevant ID.

Chapter 10.   Affiliate Marking Trends To Follow In The Present And Immediate Future

SEO

In this section, we will discuss SEO. On the off chance that you don't have the foggiest idea what SEO is, it implies website streamlining? Basically, SEO is a method for getting free traffic to your blog or site. Saying that it is a standout amongst the most ideal ways you can get more traffic. More traffic approaches more deals. That is dependably an or more when you are attempting to profit on the web.

A few people say that there is no better method for getting traffic to your site other than upgrading your SEO. Beyond any doubt paid advertisements will get you traffic significantly quicker than improving SEO. In any case, it is basic that you help your SEO from the get-go. In this part, we are going to discuss strategies you have to consider so as to expand your SEO and to get more traffic to your blog.

Having your site appear higher on the Google internet searcher is the way to progress. There are 3.5 billion quests done on Google any given day. Which implies it would be absurd of somebody to neglect SEO advancement as you would leave a great deal on the table. Despite the fact that SEO can be an extremely convoluted thing to upgrade, we will make it basic for you in this section. We will go through the essential yet best advances you have to take for you to enhance your blog and get progressively generally speaking site guests, which imply more cash in your pocket. All you will require is some additional time staring you in the face and persistence.

Backlinks

The most ideal approach to upgrade your site through SEO is beginning making backlinks. A backlink is the place you go on another blog identified with your specialty and you add a connection to your site. There's a system on the best way to do it. A great many people are splendid; they can sniff out anybody endeavoring to make backlinks. In the blogging scene, in the event that you have a messy backlink, individuals can and will erase your connection, or surprisingly more dreadful, report you.

It is basic for you to do this procedure the correct method to yield the most ideal outcomes. The best approach to make backlinks is moderately direct. To begin with, go on different websites identified with your specialty. At that point I need you to remark down on their web journals composing a section saying "Hello, I really making the most of your blog and I took in a ton from it. What's your opinion about this comparable blog entry which I read?" Then addition the connection.

You need to demonstrate that you're here to become familiar with their blog instead of advancing your blog. Making backlinks will enable you to rank higher in SEO. The more connections you have on different sites, the better the odds of Google positioning you higher up the web index. Likewise making backlinks is an extraordinary method to get free traffic to your blog, which is the most well-known path for individuals to get traffic.

Social offers

So, the subsequent stage for you to enhance your SEO is get increasingly social offers. Presently the uplifting news is, you don't have to get social offers from other individuals. You can do as such by posting your blog on Facebook gatherings and discussions identified with your specialty. Presently the main social sites I need you to advance on would be 1. Facebook bunches 2. Twitter 3. Gatherings 4. Google+. These are the top sites for you to get a huge amount of free traffic and to produce a superior upgraded SEO.

Much the same as making backlinks, you have to ensure when you're posting on these social sites or networks. Your objective ought to be to help or teach the network, as opposed to advance your blog. It is additionally suggested that you post two or three different sites incorporated into your offer, so you don't seem as though somebody advancing your blog or site.

In certain specialties, explicit Facebook gatherings or structures could have more than millions in reach. Which means it would be an incredible plan to advance your blog on their stage. Much the same as I recently referenced previously, the more connections of your sites present on different destinations the higher odds of you advancing your SEO.

Additionally recall, we will probably get much traffic to your blog as could be expected under the circumstances. Posting your web journals on the social sites and structures can enable you to create higher traffic without spending a dime. However, on the other hand ensure you are a piece of the network. Continuously remain occupied with the remarks segment helping other individuals in the network, on the off chance that you need a superior commitment rate when you post your site on the gathering or gathering.

Truth is enhancing your SEO can take years. Which implies you have to begin immediately for you streamline it to a dimension you need it to be? Despite the fact that it may take you years to augment you're SEO, that doesn't imply that you will get no traffic for quite a long time to come.

The two techniques we just talked about in this section will enable you to get free traffic from the earliest starting point and a great deal of it. You must be steady with it, which means making backlinks consistently for one hour and posting via web-based networking media stages, etc. On the off chance that you are predictable with it, at that point you ought to have no issue getting traffic throughout each and every day. In the end, Google will perceive your articles and streamline it dependent on how well your articles have been composed.

In all honesty, Google is splendid at discovering online journals which can give incredible substance. You need great substance over the long haul. The more extended your site has been available, the higher the odds of you appearing on the highest point of the Google web index dependent on watchword. So, make sure to enhance your blog entry from the earliest starting point as you will be in an ideal situation in the event that you do as such, and remain steady with it.

YouTube

YouTube is an expert with regards to promoting your site. So, in this section, we are going to discuss how to showcase your blog on YouTube. Likewise, taking advantage of this stage is essential. We will go well ordered on the best way to become your YouTube channel to the point where you are getting a significant measure of traffic to your blog.

To clear up, you needn't bother with a million endorsers for you to see achievement gaining guests to your blog. You may utilize YouTube as a device to make traffic to your essential source which would be your blog. For that, you are not required to turn into a YouTube superstar. Presently, on the off chance that you need to be a full-time YouTube, at that point go right ahead. Notwithstanding, this isn't what we will show you in this part.

We will direct you on the best way to utilize YouTube to get traffic to your blog. Contingent upon your specialty, influencing explicit recordings to can be emotional. I can't reveal to you how to make your recordings, since I have no clue what specialty your blog is about. You may need to do that exploration independent from anyone else. With that cleared up, let me tell you the best way to create more traffic from YouTube.

YouTube is a search engine

Give me a chance to ask you an inquiry. In the event that you need to learn explicit errands where do you seek? Your answer is YouTube or Google. After Google, YouTube is the most utilized web index on the web. For you to produce traffic to the site, you have to make recordings which are identified with your specialty and give data or help take care of an issue. For example, on the off chance that your blog is in the wellness specialty, at that point you can make recordings on the best way to complete a squat or how to lessen lower back torment.

As should be obvious one video gives data and the following one takes care of an issue. You need to ensure that you are transferring recordings which give data and help watchers tackle an issue. Along these lines, you can pick up their trust, in the long run, getting them to visit your blog. The primary thing you have to do is make sense of all the current issues or questions individuals may have about your specialty. At that point make a video giving data and disclosing how to fix a specific issue.

The best part about YouTube is that it is totally focused on traffic. So, you will have no issue changing over them into a confiding in crowd to your blog. To improve this progression, first, discover what your gathering of people is searching for. Second, give them the data they are seeking.

Catch watchers' data

You should ensure take you are catching however many watchers data as would be prudent. In a perfect world, you need to get their email. On the off chance that they pursue your Facebook page and buy in to your channel, that would be an incredible begin. Our essential objective, with the majority of our YouTube advertising, ought to gather watchers' messages. This will enable you to remain associated with the individual who is keen on your specialty.

At whatever point you post another blog entry, the individual who picked in to enter their email will get a notice. Enabling more watchers to your blog immediately without you doing any leg work. Most bloggers drive traffic exclusively from their email list. Presently there are numerous approaches to gather messages. The most straightforward way is given them a blessing.

Truth is everyone cherishes free stuff. For a great many people giving, out their email for a bit of free data or guide would not be a major ordeal by any means. In the later parts, I will tell you the best way to make a select in page for you to catch email. For the time being, I will examine the technique. What you need to do is after the finish of your video, I need you to state something along the line of "Hello in the event that you need a free digital book on the best way to put on muscle, clicks the connection beneath!" Once your watchers click the connection, they will be incited to enter the email to get that blessing.

When you have figured out how to gather their email, they will end up being a bought in part to your mailing list. At whatever point you post another blog; they will be informed through email and may turn into your confided in group of onlookers. These are the general population you need to offer partner items to. They will profit. All the more critically, gathering email will profit.

Honestly, you don't have to infer any techniques on the best way to present your video on get numerous perspectives. All you need is 1,000 perspectives for each video, and you will get a lot of messages exclusively from that system. Our essential objective is to gather messages of drawing in peruses, which YouTube will assist you with immensely.

Ensure you are posting incredible substance recordings at any rate once per week, and in the long run this will make a snowball impact of watchers enabling you to gather increasingly more email as you continue posting. Much the same as your articles, your YouTube recordings ought to be enlightening and all around recorded.

In addition, they should enable watchers to address their inquiry. Likewise, abstain from running advertisements on your YouTube recordings. You are utilizing YouTube exclusively for traffic, not for money. Keeping your recordings promotion unrestrained choice assistance, you achieve more watchers. Likewise, it will enable your watchers to stick around until the finish of the video. Which is fundamental for them to do, this is the place you will tell them you have a blessing to offer.

Chapter 11.   How   To   Create   A Landing Page That Converts

As a web page, the landing page is one that's meant to connect to digital ads like Facebook and Google ads. Landing page transfers the users via your sales funnel, which increases conversion rates by a high percentage.

For affiliate marketers that want to improve their rates of conversion and leads, landing pages can do the trick.

It is not easy for a business without the in-depth knowledge of useful landing pages to create one, hence a lot of affiliate markers buy landing pages off landing page builder platforms like Click Funnel. This way, they don't need to get a coding expert to do anything for them.

If you are seeking for useful landing pages, we will discuss the different places that you can access optimization tools for your landing pages.

How Landing Pages Work

Landing pages are created to work solely for the digital ads that you have placed, in a bid to get them to improve concessions. Want to heighten the returns from what you have spent on ads, you should consider landing pages.

Landing pages are mainly made via codes or using a landing page builder. The URL of the landing page is linked to the digital ad that you have placed on any ad platform.

Apart from being made to improve the message of your ad, the landing pages can't be likened to web pages since they are interested in stating a single message. Landing pages do not come with external links such as a toolbar or menu. The landing page's main aim is to nudge users to carry out a particular action that is in line with the offer of your ad.

Affiliates use landing pages in different ways, but the primary usage is in capturing important details about visitors like an email address. To get the information, a lot of landing pages come with attractive offers that visitors can't resist.

It is easy to spot a successful landing page, as it is seamlessly linked to the ad, allowing visitors to convert quickly, and dole out the information that's needed. With the information gathered, the affiliate marketers can then carry out future email marketing campaigns.

Who Are Landing Pages Right for?

Landing pages are great for affiliates that want to earn a lot from how much they spent on the ad. It is fantastic for those that want to have their ads optimized.

For anyone into PPC ads, having a successful landing page is the way forward, as it allows visitors to get what they saw on the ad quickly.

Landing pages are meant for:

Those affiliates that do not have awesome websites.

Creating a landing page is affordable and adds beauty to those sites that are outdated or not pleasing to the eyes.

Those businesses that do not have an offer on their sites.

It is rare to see a website that may have an already made webpage with the same message that your ad states. Customizing the landing pages is a great method of matching the add to whatever offers you have at hand.

Those PPC advertisers that want more control over their sales to funnel:

When they use landing pages, they minimize the normal website noise noticed in a typical site like menus.

What the landing pages offer is a more vivid on-page call to action that increases the conversion rate when compared with the usual web pages.

Your website is great. Landing pages are not designed solely for those that do not have confidence in their websites. Having a professional landing page can improve your conversion rates, as those affiliates that linked their ads to their landing pages, instead of generic web pages, notice an improvement in their conversion rate.

Landing Page Cost

Creating a landing page cost little or nothing. It doesn't cost a dime if you decide to code it yourself or make use of a free landing page builder platform.

If, on the other hand, you are looking for professional work, you can try out the top landing page builder platforms. Some charge from $25 to about $100 monthly.

On the other hand, you can try out Fiverr, and hire a freelancer to build off for you, from as little as $5 to as high as $500. It all depends on the quality of the landing pages that you are looking for.

Landing Page Providers

Leadpages

Leadpages is a landing page building platform that charges a monthly fee of $25, and it is great for those affiliates that want their landing pages, yet do not have the requisite coding knowledge.

Unbounce

It is a landing page building platform that charges a monthly fee of $79. It is great for those affiliates that want a higher level of encryption like SSL encryption.

Instapage

This landing page building platform charges a monthly fee of $99, and it is meant for those brands that want to create their landing pages immediately based on how their web design currently is.

A Marketing Agency

This costs about $300-$700+ for each landing page. There is no monthly fee, as it is just one payment.

Fiverr

On Fiverr, you can get freelancers that can build your Landing page based on your specification from $5 to over $500.

It is important that each provider comes with different packages, services, as well as user experiences.

You can also try out free landing page builders, but you may notice that they don't have customization abilities. If you use the free option, you will have to input the provider's logo. Want an effective conversion rate? You should consider using any of the paid options.

How to Create a Landing Page

Before you go about creating a landing page, you have first to choose the platform for you. You should then pen down your goals, choose the right call to action, pen down your copy, have your ad designed, as well as link the ad to your Landing page.

Once you follow these steps, you will have an effective landing page in no time.

Choose the Right Landing Page Platform to use

Whatever landing page platform that you opt for is where your landing page will be built. For those that have decided to create their landing pages via code, they may have to do so using the back end of the website.

As for those that are not developing theirs themselves, they do not need to have the necessary web knowledge to create a landing page. All they need is a landing page builder such as Leadpages or Instapage.

Few people know how to code, hence there is a great chance that you may need a landing page builder platform.

What Is Your Goal

Creating a landing page comes with its goal, but the major goal rotates round your conversion objective. It could be event registration, downloads, or lead collection.

Whatever your landing page goal is should match with your ad goal. When you use your ad goal to design the landing page, it is easier to reach your goal. If you decide to make use of a landing page builder, opt for the template that works well with your brand, as well as the goal.

Choose a Call to Action

The CTA of your landing page should match that of your ad. Let's say, you write 'get a free membership now' in your ad, and in your landing page, you write, 'get a paid membership now', then there is a big problem.

If you try such with a platform like Facebook, it sees it as a type of deceptive marketing practice. As a penalty, it has your ad rejected, and your account closed.

Pen Down a Catchy Headline

The headline on your landing page should be similar to the one on your ad. Make your headline catchy and repeat to them the reason they are on your landing page. When you remind them, converting them becomes easier? It is important to note that when creating your landing page, especially the mobile version, it comes with restricted space. You have to keep the headline brief. If you write a long thing, only a few words will be seen by your visitors.

Look for Supporting Media

Don't leave your landing page looking bland. It is advisable to add a visual to improve its appealing nature to the eyes. If you want your ad's message to sit well with your visitors, then make it appealing.

A lot of people make use of images on their landing pages, but you can take it up a notch, and use video instead.

It doesn't matter what media you decide to use; the quality has to be high and must be in line with your brand and ad's goal.

Opt for a Simple Contact Form

Your landing page shouldn't have so much information. The same should be said for the contact form that you put there. Avoid trying to ask for a lot of contact info from your visitors because they may be discouraged to give any. Ask for little as possible and watch them convert. Let's say you want to send them a free eBook; what you should ask for is their name and email address, nothing more. Don't go ahead asking for their address, or phone number.

Have Your Landing Page Linked to Your Ad?

If you want the ad clicks to direct your visitors to your landing page, your ad's URL has to be updated with the landing page's URL.

For those that are churning out their landing page themselves via code, they can opt for their custom URL. Those that are making use of a landing page builder can easily have their URL generated. They can then copy and paste the URL.

How To Link your Landing Page to Google Ads

If you have decided to link a Google ad to the landing page, you will begin by gaining access to your Google Ads account.

Choose the corresponding campaign, before you head to Ads.

Get your Ads Updated in Google Ads.

Now, you will see where you can have the URL of the previous ads updated. You should then have a new ad created or duplicate the old one. At this point, put in the new URL.

Have your existing Google Ad edited?

Have the URL in the Google Ads updated?

How To Link your Landing Page to Facebook Ads?

If you want to link a Facebook Ad to the landing page, you need first to check if the landing page is not flouting any Facebook's ad policies.

Once this is done, head to the Facebook Ads Manager account.

You will see on the right side of your screen, the 'Ads' tab, press it.

While at the Ads page, you can easily have a new ad created by clicking on the 'Create' button. You can also have an old and updated by clicking on it.

How to edit an old Facebook ad, or create a new one.

If you have decided to create a new one, you can use the prompts. If, on the other hand, you have decided to update an old ad, copy and then paste the URL of the landing pages, then press "Publish." It will save.

Input Analytics Tracking to Landing Page

If you want to track the performance of your landing page, you have to input data, as well as for analytics tracking to the page.

You can use any analytics tool of your choice, be it the free Google Analytics or Heap.

If you decide to use a tracking tool, it will give you a code, which you should enter into the landing page code.

If you have decided to make use of a website builder, the code should be pasted into the spot that is created for analytics tracking.

Have Your Landing Page Optimized?

Immediately the landing page is now functioning; you have to monitor and optimize it continuously. The ad settings, keywords, and audience have to be improved regularly.

When you make use of the data gathered from your landing page, you can easily find out those areas of the ads that need to be updated.

How to optimize your landing page:

Segment the landing page by traffic source:

Your target audience is made up of different people with different needs. It is your job to segment those in your audience through the ads and ensures that your landing pages have been altered to meet those people that convert.

Use different offers:

It won't be a bad idea to create campaigns with different offers, as it allows you to know which of them is more effective when it comes to capturing leads.

Have Your Color Scheme Adjusted?

Do you know that the hue affects the level of conversion? Some hues work better than others. You should try out which one will work well for you.

Alter the image

Sometimes, you may think an image is the right one for your landing page, but it isn't. The performance of an image should determine if it stays or should be changed. Don't keep on an image that's not performing because you like it.

Add urgency

One thing that gets people to respond is when they think that there are limited offers of something. You can also make it seem that there's a limited amount of time too. You will be surprised by how it drives conversion.

Adjust sales copy:

At first, you may not know if you are underselling or underselling, but you can know for sure if your sales copy regularly. This allows you to discuss how great you are or not.

Add testimonials:

A lot of people tend to trust brands or affiliated when they add testimonials or reviews to their landing page. This can aid in increasing your conversion rate. You should try out different testimonials to see which one is working well.

Use Two Landing Pages At The Same Time
Different landing pages invoke different effects. To know which is more effective, you should try out an experiment with two landing pages.

To have your landing pages optimized, you should try and adjust during a period. It allows you to know which part of the landing page is great or which one needs changes.

Let's say, if you altered your picture and headline at the same time, you may not know which one of them led to an improvement in conversions.

If you decided to change the CTA or offer, don't forget to alter your ad copy too.

Landing Page Characteristics That Every Successful Landing Page Has
Each landing page out there may be unique, but it has some characteristics that make it successful. They are:

Right Landing Page Structure

Those pages that barely convert usually have a thing in common. Those landing pages are not properly organized when it comes to their information flow.

What the owners of those landing pages think is that they have to religiously stick to a logical top-to-bottom structure, which begins with talking about the concept, and comes to a halt with using a call-to-action button. Using this format won't give you the desired result.

The truth remains that few visitors even scroll down to the bottom of the listing. We live in a fast-paced world, where no one has the patience to move down. We want information now! Not later!

If you want to convert, put the best features on top, as well as the necessary information. This prevents your visitors from ignoring an important fact.

Some affiliates may feel that placing their call-to-action (CTA) on top of the page is weird, but it works magic.

Use Targeted Headline

When a person visits a landing page, the first thing that meets her eyes is the headline of the landing page. What this means is that you should put a lot of thoughts to the headline of the landing page. Don't make it an afterthought.

Studies have shown that using any of the following can give you the high converting headline.

- Make use of numbers,
- Try out between five to nine words,
- Make your intentions clear, and
- <u>Use multiple parts.</u>

When you incorporate these characteristics, you will be surprised at the level of how your conversion rate.

Use Proper Colors

A lot of people feel that the color scheme that one uses should be based on his or her preference, but that's far from reality. If you want your landing page to be ranked among the high converting ones, you should look at the following:

- Red translates to bold and exciting;
- Orange means warmth, as well as clarity;
- Blue translates to strength and dependability;
- Green means vitality, money, and growth;
- Purple translates to imagination and creativity;
- White means calm and neutral.
- <u>Purple translates to imagination and creativity.</u>

From the above, you can tell that each hue evokes different feelings and emotions. Hues have a way of affecting a person's behavior subconsciously.

Credibility and Approval

Gone are those days when landing pages were created to be all about sales. Now, your landing page has to come off as natural, if you want to succeed. What you should do is create a landing page that allows your visitors to decide for themselves based on what you have created. It shouldn't be about you trying to force your product down their throats.

One way to get this done is by utilizing social proof.

Examples are reviews, testimonials, as well as case studies. When you incorporate these in your landing page, you come off as being more credible. Before you know it, your visitors are making the needed purchases.

Chapter 12.   Growing An Email List

So far, you have learned what affiliate marketing is, what its benefits and pros and cons are, as well as how you can become a successful marketer, find your right niche, and approach brands. You pretty much know how to get started. Now, it is time to delve deep and expand your business as an affiliate marketer.

The number one priority when building an online business is building an email list. Imagine that 20% of all your work brings 80% of the profits like the 80/20 principle. Building an email list is similar to 80% benefits. Any successful entrepreneur will advise you that mistakes are a part of the learning process. However, if there is one thing they can go back in time and do, it would be to start building an email list sooner. Once your website has been created and set up, start by collecting emails by offering forms to the visitors to sign up.

The email list is a business's most important asset as it is the prime connection to their subscribers. It is about maintaining direct relationships. If there are 50,000 people who subscribe to your website and they are not concerned about your company or your product then your list might not be worth it. Even worse, it may cost you money. A monthly fee would be taken by your service provider based on the number of subscribers. Therefore, the actual assets of the company are the ones who are engaged with the products. They are the people who are interested in purchasing your product or services. You have to focus on building a list of quality subscribers rather than the merely focusing on the quantity. What matters is how you maintain a good relationship with your subscribers. Many marketers might disagree, saying it's safer to have a list with a large number of subscribers. However, a smaller list of quality subscribers who engage with the website is better than a big list of mostly uninterested customers.

Importance of growing your email list:

Here are several reasons why it is important to have an email list:

1. Your Facebook, Instagram, or Twitter followers might be thousands in number, but since these platforms do not belong to you, you have no control over your main assets. If one of these platforms were to shut down one day, all your connections to your customers are lost. If you have a website that belongs to you, the email list belongs to you automatically. However, you must keep your list backed up regularly. An Excel document or a cloud storage service, such as Dropbox, can be used for storage. They might just be a list of emails, but it is worth more than you know.

2. Email is a direct connection to your target audience. It can help in building rapport and maintaining relationships with them. An effective way to understand the needs, desires, and pains of your audience is by surveying them through email. Engaging

in a conversation with your subscribers can always help you in finding out which product or service needs to be focused on. This can also let them be aware of your product. Features like notifications on the publication of new articles and promotions will encourage them to visit your website more often.

3. It is the most cost effective and beneficial way to provide true value to customers who are interested. Emails are a free channel for promoting products to an audience that is already into your business. It is a free means of product promotion and has the highest conversion rate when compared to any other promotional channel. Therefore, building a list of engaged subscribers will always help you build a much stronger and profitable business.

4. An email list can help create partnerships within the industry. It will be easier because you have the exposure to your audience to offer. You will be well appreciated in your field if you can help gain visibility towards an interesting market.

How to grow your email list

The process of gathering email addresses is effortless. All it requires is an option where the visitors of your website can give their information, like name, email address, etc., and a marketing service to collect, store, and arrange the information. Generally, people are not so keen on giving away their personal information. It is your responsibility to convince them through the website that the information is given for a good reason. A free gift can be offered in exchange for their information. This practice is called a lead magnet. Let's explore this in detail.

Your first task would be to find the right system to organize these emails. An email marketing system will collect, store, organize, and create automated messages. They can also be used to split test and track campaign information. These services are mostly charged on a monthly basis or will depend on the number of subscribers. The cost will be increased as the number increases. When choosing an email management provider, certain conditions should be examined.

Automation:

A feature that automates messages according to a given date and time is very important.

Segmentation:

When you can segment subscribers based on preferences and interests, it improves the efficiency of your campaigns. For instance, you can separate people who have subscribed and received a free gift from the people who signed up for more services. Therefore, you can manage different campaigns for each segment based on their preferences.

A/B testing:

This feature is vital to improving your marketing strategies for a successful business. A/B testing can help send one type of email (A) to half of your audience and another type of email (B) to the other half. You can observe which type has the best results. You can see the percentage of subscribers who opened the mail or clicked a link in the mail. The difference between the two types will be the subject line, the text, the product, etc. Testing helps you optimize the way your campaign functions and benefits your business. Here are three recommended email marketing services you can start out with:

I) AWeber.com: This is quite an affordable option and also a complete management system. Its elements are automation, tracking, and subscriber segmentation. It has a simple interface and provides customer care support every day. Their website includes video tutorials that explain the different features it has. You will have access to all the features, regardless of the plan you choose. For up to 500 subscribers, $19 is the monthly fee (at the time this book is being written).

II) MailChimp.com: This is a very popular and simple email marketing service. They include a free plan for up to 2000 subscribers, which is a good place to start for beginners. This free plan only includes a few of the basic features required. You can upgrade as your budget increases. It is convenient as it will allow you to collect email addresses right after you install it.

The paid plan gives you access to A/B testing, full data campaigns, which are all, required to run a successful campaign. The service also provides you with video tutorials on how to use their features. It also comes with live customer support, but it's available only for the paid plan.

III) GetResponse.com: The basic plan is $15 per month, and it gives you access to all the features required to start a business. The user interface is quite simple to get around, whereas the video tutorials are easy to understand. It includes 24/7 customer care live chat and assistance over email or phone. The sign-up forms and landing pages they provide are quite appealing. With an extra $15, you will have access to unlimited landing pages.

The lead magnet

You have definitely come across forms that state, "subscribe to our newsletter," on several websites. You would probably not be bothered by it unless the website has to provide information that you don't want to miss out on. On the other hand, if they were to provide you with a free gift of high value, you would give away your email address. For this particular gift to be considered important, it has to be something that your customers need. If you have done the proper research required, then you already know what your audience prefers. This gift should be something that is a solution to the issues similar to solution your paid product provides. This high-value offer should not be expensive or time-consuming to prepare. It just has to solve the problem.

For instance, a fitness instructor is selling an online program for men who want to increase their muscle mass. The free gift should be a cheat sheet that provides a sneak peek into what the website will provide. This information will land an email address for sure. To see this cheat sheet as having an increased value, it has to be a well-designed PDF, with images of exercise.

Therefore, a lead magnet can be different things:

- An eBook
- An audio file
- A video tutorial
- A short course
- A cheat sheet
- A free live video consultation

These freebies can be delivered at your doorstep or through an email address, for instance, a short video course in three parts. This approach is practical because it builds a connection with the subscribers. They will look forward to the next video in the series and will get used to your emails in their inbox. One important factor is that the freebie should be relevant to the product that you're selling. Your subscribers are only great if they become potential buyers or brand advocates.

In the last example provided, the trainer gives a cheat sheet as a freebie and the paid product was the online fitness programs. Let's say the trainer gave away a video game as the incentive. This is obviously not relevant to the product. There is no reason to convince yourself that the person opting for the video game would purchase the fitness program. It is because the two programs are not related.

The sign-up form

The sign-up form is the actual form that the visitors to the website use to enter their name and email address. It can be placed in strategic locations to optimize the number of people who sign up. Your marketing service would provide several templates that would be easy to customize and edit. You have to choose a form that matches your brand and looks professional.

The headline to your form should state the service you provide and a solution. It should also mention what they would receive as a result of signing up. It's always a good idea to lay it out in bullet points. For instance, a heading may say, "five easy exercises for the upper body." Then, the details, such as its benefits, should be provided in a short message format that should be easily understood at a glance. Make sure to use the right font size and colors that suit your brand design. It should also stand out on the website.

There will be a call-to-action button on the form that plays a vital role. It mostly contains instructions to a visitor on what to do next. It is better to use words other than "subscribe," and choose a more beneficial verb. "Download now" or "get access now" are some examples that have been proven to give good results. Moreover, make sure that the button stands out, so give it a contrasting color to attract attention.

The placement of the sign-up form on the web page can make a big difference in conversion. Your website must be designed to achieve the maximum number of email lists. For this, there are places in which the forms, when positioned, can increase the chance of the visitors turning into subscribers.

Above the fold:

This is the portion where the visitor arrives on your site, even before navigating it. Use a feature box that fills up the entire screen. This helps convert all the visitors into subscribers very easily as long as the free gift is exciting enough.

The upper right sidebar:

This is one of the most common places to add it.

Above the top menu:

Within WordPress, there is a free plugin called "Hello Bar" that gives a thin horizontal form above the web page's top navigation menu.

After each blog post:

Once a person has read one of your articles to the end, he or she has just demonstrated an interest in your content. This is the kind of person who forms your audience base, and you would want this person to join the mailing list. Therefore, you have to place the form right after the post. If you offer a freebie, you will get a better result. It could be an action plan or a checklist that compliments your article. For example, if the article is about content marketing, a freebie could be five interesting headline templates.

At the beginning of each post:

If you write long articles, there is a possibility where you can give an option to download it as a PDF version, which they can print or save for later. It's always considered to be a safe tactic that works wonders. The reader would then enter the email address to download it.

Pop-up forms: This can be a bit annoying most of the time, but somehow, it always gets good results. After using pop-up options, marketers have noticed a 30% to 1000% increase in the number of email subscribers when compared to the simple sidebar format. WPBeginner.com tried this out on their website and found a 600% increase in the number of email subscribers. To make them less annoying, there are few changes you can make. At first, make sure the pop up appears only after ten or sixty seconds after the visitor has landed on the page. It is less intrusive this way, as the visitor will be able to review the information he or she is looking for.

A visitor recognition pop-up software is another approach to address this concern. This allows the pop up to appear just once if it's a first-time visitor, and they won't be interrupted every single time. You could also provide an exit-intent pop up that appears only when the visitor is about to leave the page, that is when the cursor nears the exit tab. Do not use pop-ups on every single page on your website. Choose to use them on pages with the most traffic.

The landing page or the sales page is an interruption-free web page to which you direct traffic for a sole purpose. For example, it could be used to market one product or to collect different email addresses. We call it interruption-free because there is a link, navigation menu, or sidebar that could distract the visitor from the action he or she wants to take. There will only be one call to action button — download, log in, sign up or get access — and some sales pitch to convince the visitor to do something.

You can use this landing page as the destination page, which can send visitors from social media or elsewhere to increase the chance of changing into email subscribers. You can send them to this landing page rather than the homepage. A sales page can directly be placed on your WordPress landing page using the plugin. There are also premium landing page builders that include such features as testing and gathering information. These templates will be proven to perform well when it comes to converting. The most preferred ones are LeadPages.com, OptimizePress.com, and InstaPage.com.

Chapter 13.   Managing Your Life As An Affiliate Marketer

One of the big issues for many affiliate marketers and people who work from home in general is time management. We all tend be lazy and procrastinate and, when there is no boss to answer to and no deadlines waiting, the time tends to fly by and the work tends not to get done.

If you are actually going to make it as an affiliate marketer, make no mistake, it will require many hours of hard work before you are making enough money where you can be sure you have a steady income coming in. Even then, you will always want to grow your business and, instead of working shorter days than you would at a normal job, you should actually work longer days, as you have all the comfort of your home around you and working 10-12 hours a day is something you should try to get used to. The comfort of the home with no bosses around is actually the downfall of many online workers, so I have decided to address some common issues people face when working from home and discuss some possible ways of getting rid of these issues.

The Internet

The Internet is your playground as an affiliate marketer, so there is certainly no way of not being online when you are working. But we all know how many distractions there are on the Internet nowadays. What is worse, many of these distractions such as

Facebook, Twitter and YouTube will be integral parts of your work, which means you will have to be visiting them. The trick here is not to use your personal profiles much while working. You should have social pages set up for your business and really avoid spending much time chatting on Facebook with your friends or retweeting the Lol Catz on Twitter. Make sure your friends know when your working hours are and get them to respect that. While working from home does allow for some distractions, spending much time on the Internet doing random stuff will quickly eat away at your working hours and limiting the time you waste on the Internet will be one of the most important factors to keep track of. If necessary, there are even software apps you can use to limit yourself from using the websites that take away most of your time.

Say No to Real-Life Distractions

When people know you work from home, they will think that means you can always be there for them. Whether they just need someone to chill with on their day off or need your help getting stuff done, you will often end up receiving relentless calls to do stuff. You will have to learn to say no to such calls and set yourself up with some kind of working hours, otherwise the time will get away from you.

Sleep can be a big problem, as well. When you are so close to your bed, taking a nap may seem like a great idea in the middle of the day. It never really is other than if you are too exhausted to work, which should not be the case too often. Always remind yourself that your future lies on what you make as an affiliate marketer and this is now your profession, so treat it as you would any other job and do not get distracted by random things while working.

Free Days

Like anyone else, you need days off. While there are no bosses to tell you when to work or when not to, make sure you set yourself some goals. If you have had a good productive week, take the weekend completely off and have some fun with friends or take an enjoyable trip to the countryside to clear your head. It can really help put things into perspective and get you back on track to work full hours the next day. Remember to take free days and your mind and body will thank you for it.

Keep the Optimism

Affiliate marketing can be a slow business at first, so keeping a positive attitude about it and remembering that success will come if you give it enough time and effort is important if you don't want to lose motivation. Lack of motivation can be an end to your career before it has even really started, so remember to keep optimistic even when things are not going smoothly. As you know, this is something you can make money at, it just takes time. You may want to enlist friends to help you with this or join online communities of affiliate marketers where you can feed on the success stories of others while slowly building one of your own.

Organizing the Work

Keeping well organized is the secret to success in any work and affiliate marketing is no different. Especially with this line of work, there will be many different tasks to complete, from creating content, finding programs, linking your content up, optimizing your websites for search engines, sending mailers ,and all sorts of other things, it will be easy to get disorganized and lose track of what is done and what is yet to be done. Keep notes on all the tasks you need to complete and set yourself realistic daily goals to meet. Make sure you don't go to bed before your to-do list is complete for the day.

Expanding Your Business

Affiliate marketing is a business that can be easily expanded in many directions. For starters, you will usually be working alone but, as time goes on, many opportunities will arise to expand the business. The one thing that drives affiliate business is fresh content. There are many websites on the Internet where you can purchase content relatively cheap and, once you start making money with affiliate business, this is a great way to reinvest money. New content along with the old will keep making money and the profits should just keep going up and up.

Successful affiliate marketers often have dozens of websites and it can take many writers to keep it all updated. There is no reason ever to stop expanding. The limit in affiliate marketing is really only your ambition and the dedication you have for the job.

Conclusion

Affiliate marketing is an industry that keeps changing, and for that reason, you must always be ready to explore new possibilities. It is important to discover new opportunities for you to increase your income.

For individuals who are thinking of setting up an affiliate marketing, think no more. The internet is a great platform where you can make your business succeed as well as compete with the rest. You only need to have a great website and convert it into a profitable one. Before you move on to sign up for an affiliate network, it is better if you already have an existing website that generates a steady flow of web traffic. This will give you an upper hand because you already have an audience on the internet.

To boost your position as a prospective partner, make sure you include effective marketing techniques such as brand marketing, search engine optimization, social media marketing, and influencer marketing.

Above all, make sure that you create relevant and quality content. Also, your content should address the needs of your audience. You can make a huge profit from affiliate marketing but only when you are patient and committed to following the right path. Remember. Many people have joined affiliate marketing, but only a few are enjoying the profits that come with affiliate marketing. So be smart and focus on giving your audience value. Over time, you will start to reap the many benefits that come with affiliate marketing.

It is my hope that after reading this book you will have a general understanding of how affiliate marketing works in principal, what niches are and how to pick the right one for yourself, how to create SEO content and how to market your content to potential customers. Following all the tips and tricks from this book should set you well on your way towards becoming a well-established and serious affiliate marketer with a bright future on the horizon for you.

The information given in this book is not only meant for enlightening you on the intricacies of the field but also to warn the novice players to make informed decisions over ad judgment calls. I hope you found this book useful and informative.

www.ingramcontent.com/pod-product-compliance
Lightning Source LLC
Chambersburg PA
CBHW070347220526
45467CB00001B/283